WITHIN
THE
HEART OF LOVE

BOOK 3

A Spiritual Memoir by Dee Delaney

Wrate's Publishing

Within the Heart of Love (The Truth is Within, Book 3)

Published in 2023 by Wrate's Publishing

ISBN 978-1-7393758-4-3

Edited and typeset by Wrate's Editing Services
www.wrateseditingservices.co.uk

This is a second edition. The first edition was published in 2019 by Garnet Press.

Dedicated to Magda,
You touched so many hearts

Contents

How do you show the world the light is within?
You write the book and tell your story.

Introduction

I started out on my journey of self-discovery when I sat in silence for the first time in my life and turned inward. I had to stop running from myself and face the pain I was holding onto. My life fell apart when my husband died suddenly, leaving me alone with 2 children to raise. My grief was compounded by the deaths of my father, two ex-partners, and a close friend; it was a lot to deal with. As I struggled to make sense of life, I began questioning why I was surrounded by so much death, believing there was something inherently wrong with me. It wasn't until I surrendered to the silence inside that I realised the grief I was experiencing was not for them; it was for me. You see, I had abandoned myself so completely in my search for love, giving love to everyone and everything outside of myself until there was nothing left for me. Well, not quite nothing. There was still a spark of light inside my heart that whispered, 'I am here', and from that moment on, it guided me home, and gave me the courage to be who I am today.

Everything changed after I connected to the truth within.

I moved to a small fishing village in South Goa, India, and with the support of the local community, rebuilt my life. As I journeyed deeper into the heart of my being, the flickering embers of light grew brighter. My adventures took me across the globe, from East to West, where I found pieces of myself buried in different lands. As I followed my heart, and the calling from within, I began to transform from the inside out, learning to ride the waves of change with grace and ease, no longer fighting the demons inside my mind. As I danced with nature, the forces within swept the old me away.

The new me emerged through my writing. She guided me through stories of the past and to reclaim the memories of those who had walked before: transmuting the pain inside my heart; recalling suffering from the Burning Times; bringing the Christed perspective back to life, forgiving the past and creating more space for love inside my heart.

As I shine light on these times, may my words bring passion and feelings to the surface of your being, as they did for me when I wrote them. We all have a unique path in life; it is ours to walk freely. I share my story, in the hope that together we can learn from our mistakes and rewrite a brighter future for us all.

Big love always,

Dee

THE WAY OF LOVE

This journey we walk together in our own unique way
is the soul's search for love that will always stay.
It is the ancient story of the sacred marriage within,
of Spirit and Soul, as she searches for him.

A story retold throughout time
as myth, as legend, now being remembered as mine.
A woman who left her struggles behind,
who sees herself through her heart that shines.

I left the West and moved to the East
where Mother India held space for me to find peace.
I walked through the darkness and found light in her place,
opening doorways to another time and space.

But my path to healing had only just begun,
As I turned inward there was more to come.
This path that led me into the heart of the Divine
has been taught by ancient sages since the dawn of time.

It is the path of Unity that bears no strife,
and is represented symbolically by the 'Tree of Life'.
A metaphor for the steps we need to take,
to activate the body as our higher selves awake.

Rooted in grace by the Goddess Divine,
She's rewriting the story for our time.
As my soul journeyed into the great cosmic womb,
it was there in the darkness that I started to bloom.

I travelled back to the UK and trained as a Soul Midwife
where I discovered my heavenly connection to the afterlife.
As I parted the veils and looked into the abyss,
I found the light that always exists.

It is here in this book that I bid you farewell,
as I hand over the story for the Goddess to tell.
She teaches us mysteries from East and from West,
and through our own sexuality, which is sacred, best.

Initiates searching for the elixir of life
discover it when the masculine unites with his beloved wife.
This ignites the triple flame of Christ Consciousness,
which opens our hearts to all of Oneness.

May you be blessed by the greatest love story of time,
as spirit and soul meet in the heart of the divine.

When you step into the heart of love, you enter a world of awareness where creation resides. As you hear and register *all of yourself* as this awareness, you are then able to hear and register someone else with the same depths as yourself. It is this depth that you bring to yourself and subsequently share with others that makes life so rich and beautiful because, when you see beyond the veil of misunderstanding, you find so much love and compassion for your fellow beings. This *Way of Love* asks you to keep the heart open, especially through the hardships in life, as you accept what is without trying to change it. It asks you to forgive yourself and others as you venture out into the world, learning from past mistakes so that, in time, you are able to see with new meaning and clarity. When you learn by living, by making mistakes, and by succeeding in life, you grow and expand into a greater version of who you are. You just have to put one foot in front of the other and live your life one moment at a time, knowing that you have everything you need to achieve the best life imaginable if you turn inward and listen to your heart. However, many people have forgotten that the secret to vitality and happiness comes from awareness inside themselves, and instead, they turn to other people or things outside themselves to fill the void they feel inside. This book and everything I share are designed to help you reconnect with this awareness. It can be expressed as simply as:

Be Good. Do Good. Keep the Faith. Have Fun.

As you transcend the world of duality, the Universal Law of Love requires that you honour that which is good and resist that which is evil. Love offers the path of least resistance through duality because it nurtures your awareness *and does not create a force against life.* When there is zero force, what remains is only love. You see, if you actively resist the things you don't like, you unknowingly strengthen your awareness of what you do not want. It's a bit like how weight training strengthens muscles. If you push and fight against something, it just makes it stronger. So, if you think, say, or act out against the things you do not want, *you actively feed the energy that creates them.* But if you allow the things you don't like to flow through your awareness without holding on to or suppressing them, they will naturally dissipate on their own. In each and every moment, you have the power to transmute all the misunderstandings of the world you live in, into love. That's how simple life is and how powerful you are.

Yet, in society today, people often say things without realising they are spewing their pain out into the world, hurting themselves and others. This is because they don't have the tools to deal with some of the painful feelings that are locked inside their bodies, their minds and their souls. Many of these deep-seated feelings have been bubbling away since the beginning of time. If you allow yourself to step into your heart and feel everything without acting out the trauma, you will create a world of peace that most people on Earth truly desire. Connect to the energy that sits behind the words and turn inward. Find the part of you that is calling in the experience that is presented in front of you; it needs to be revealed and healed. When you are willing to see, hear, and feel it all—the seen and the unseen—when you are able to step beyond your own story—the shame, blame, and vulnerability—you will find love, and you will transmute your pain into more love.

This essence of *connection to yourself and to others* is the golden thread that runs throughout my book trilogy, *The Truth is Within*. When you come home to the story of love, which weaves itself through the very fabric of life, you return to your *original wholeness or true nature*. This is about acting from a place of goodness, where you feel a connection to nature, to your own divine grace, and to other people. It means seeing the world with new eyes, hearing with new ears, and loving from a higher heart. When you live from the heart, you live from a place of ultimate compassion and forgiveness for yourself first, then others. You therefore live *within the heart of love*, in union with the world around you, understanding that every experience that comes to you *comes from you*. You live in a holographic universe, where the world is a projection of your inner being. For many people, this concept might well prove to be a profound new way of seeing themselves and the universe, but as I explain throughout this book, the principle behind it is actually supported by science, philosophy and cosmic law.

It's something that many ancient civilisations knew about, but this wisdom has been lost to today's society as we've become less interested in our true selves and our inner worlds and more interested in the material world outside of ourselves, which is driven by power, greed and control. When you see the universe from this new place of reality, you become a great mirror of wisdom, both for yourself and others. You see struggle and failure as an opportunity to grow and heal. Rather than protecting and defending your mistakes righteously, you turn inward, connect to the pain, and move through it. As you journey deeper into your heart, you connect to universal consciousness, or energy, where all things reside. This connection is infinite, so there is no end ... just the continuing spiral that brings you ever closer to your inner self.

To look back on life with such love, and understanding for all that has been, is, the ultimate gift you can give yourself. So too are the people and events that enter your life to trigger you. These people, who are often vilified for their actions, touch upon the unseen, poking at memories stuck inside, sometimes, from lives that are long gone. These people and events act in your divine play to help you grow and expand, even if it may not feel like it at the time. Instead of reacting to external stimuli when triggered, if you pause and turn inward, there is always an invitation to go deeper into who you are. When you do this, something remarkable happens inside of yourself: an immense love that is hidden behind the memories of the past, is unlocked within. These memories hold profound wisdom that you've been holding onto since the beginning of time. When you drop into your body and allow these cellular memories to come to the forefront of your being, they float up and out of you, creating space for a new you to be born within. Beyond the memory is a love that purifies and heals. This juice, this source of creation inside of you, is available for free, in every moment that you tap into your body and connect to all that you are.

The memories of the past are now calling to be healed. Stories of ownership and control, division and conquest that you unknowingly keep alive in the cells of your bodies are coming to the surface to be seen. I feel it all around. The unseen is ready to be seen. And it's not pretty. But you already exist on a higher plane of reality, so you have the wisdom to deal with this pain. The question is, can you bring your body along for the ride? This battle between heart and mind is taking place inside of you, and you get to choose which way it ends. Can you let go of the stories of the past, and untangle yourself from the old narrative that is keeping you small? Can you choose love over fear? Can you ignore others and do what feels right for you? Can you hear the voice of truth beyond the lies? Can you stand your own ground, even if this means standing alone? These are the questions you will face on the road ahead as you transcend the thinking mind and step into the feeling heart. And the power to do this lies within you. One by one, you will bring about transformation and change, and this will ripple out into the world around you.

The entire universe and beyond are there to teach you and help your soul evolve. It's all part of the journey of spiritual awakening, a process of freeing yourself from limiting beliefs, thoughts and patterns so your true nature as a spiritual being can be revealed. I write about the awakening process in this book, sharing my personal story, to help others open up to theirs. I didn't really know what was happening to me at the time, even though I had read all about spiritual awakenings in hundreds of self-help books. But reading about something and actually experiencing it are two very different things. Looking back now, I can see how spiritually immature I was and how my awakening came from a place of real innocence inside. I was just being me, living my life, travelling the world, writing my books, and having fun; I was simply hoping that one day someone would pick up my work so I could create a better world for myself, and others. I dreamed of being a successful writer and worked hard at it, whilst trying to be the best version of myself. It's only now, eight years on, after returning home to the UK, that I can look back in hindsight and bring a new perspective to this work. That's because it takes time to embody spiritual wisdom, time for the mind to drop its limiting thoughts, behaviours and patterns. It is time for the physical body to detox and activate the awareness that is dormant inside. Time is needed to process it all because the shift into higher realms of consciousness is so profound that if it happened all at once, it would blow most people's circuits.

I feel it's helpful to share a little bit about the writing process itself before I get into the story, as the process was an integral part of why I awakened. Many people might perceive my books as being channelled, as if I accessed wisdom from an entity outside myself. But this is not so. When I wrote these books, I connected to a version of myself, outside of time and space. This version of me, whom I know as Sahra, represents the Child of Unity, the innocence of my true nature. She's like an ascended version of me, who has laid the foundations for the path I am walking because she remembers the Way of Love. Her presence reminded me of my own innate power, which opened me up to the experiences that brought my story to life. For my part, I committed to show up at 5 am every morning, to open my heart and allow the stream of words to flow through me. It didn't matter how tired I was, I showed up without fail, with a big pot of coffee by my side. I said a prayer, asking for clarity of mind and for the words to show me the way. And it was in the liminal space betwixt and between, I quickly found my voice. The writing process was deeply visceral and the purity of the words and how they made me feel often overwhelmed and reduced me to tears. The energy that flowed through me purified my mind and body and these beautiful books found a life of their own through faith and love that came from my heart. Of course, I wasn't aware of any of this at the time, but others who knew me saw my transformation. I seemed to be illuminated from the inside out as this presence stayed with me during the school runs and for most of the day. I eventually transformed physically, mentally and spiritually through the writing process, at times barely recognising the new person I had become.

I don't think anyone in their right mind could have predicted I would one day write a trilogy of spiritual books and publish them in the space of only a year. It didn't seem humanly possible, but that's exactly what I did. It was as if time stood still and I achieved the impossible task in the shortest amount of time. Looking back on it now, I know a higher 'force' was at play. This connection to my higher self, guided me through this initial phase of awakening into the second phase where I transcended suffering and started to embody the Christ Consciousness.

I soon discovered that my story, like many others, is part of the collective awakening that is occurring now on Earth, and will affect the whole of humanity for years to come. My particular path, chosen by my soul, was to follow in the footsteps of those ancient ones who walked before me. I was literally walking The Way of Love, reclaiming parts of me from the land as I travelled across India, France, Scotland and Bali experiencing epiphanies, discovering ancient secrets and realising miracle healing. I was helped along the way by many amazing people connected to the story that was unfolding through us all. The physical toll on my body was at times extreme. My stomach was covered in rashes, from the light purging toxins and density out of my body. My ears often crackled and popped as my consciousness experienced higher planes of reality. My eyesight went out of focus as I gained dimensional sight and glimpsed into the unseen world with my physical eyes. I started to feel energy running through my hands, energy that could be used to help others. I learnt to smell like a sniffer dog and became particularly sensitive to the aromas of sacred oils that were used in ancient times. The stream of divine energy that ran through me found its voice, in my words, but also in my body.

My friends and family at home in the UK had no idea what I had been through during the past 7 years. I found it hard to explain the unexplainable in linear words and knew the timing wasn't right for most people. Besides, I hadn't quite integrated my awakening, and without integration, I couldn't bring these complex experiences into simple, everyday language. I consequently spent a lot of time alone, with my son, popping out into the world every now and again as I adjusted to the new me. Learning to walk with this new awareness was literally like learning to walk again. There were times when I was scared by the enormity of what was happening within me. To say it felt biblical sounds a bit dramatic, but when you read the book, you'll realise I'm not far from the mark. I never quite appreciated how wet behind the ears I was when it came to spiritual maturity and soon realised that awakening is not for the faint-hearted. It revealed a part of me that was not so pretty, and that was hard. I had to deal with many aspects of myself that I had avoided and denied, experiencing intense fear, jealousy, anger and grief along the way. There was a lot of letting go as I released the beliefs' patterns and habits that no longer served me. This wasn't easy, but it was something I had to do to create space for new growth and transformation. By living my life authentically, doing the things I loved and having fun, I actually managed to transform my life while still remaining reasonably 'normal': well, normal for me!

I was shown how powerful we are as creator beings after going through my own extraordinary 'near-death' experience when my consciousness returned to God and rebirthed again. I literally felt connected to everything, everywhere, all at once. This led to a lot of internal confusion, and I had to learn to integrate the insights and experiences from my spiritual journey into my everyday life. I realised I was still holding on to so many beliefs and childhood insecurities that were getting in the way of my bliss, but I was no longer suffering in the way I had in the past.

Even though I have been on this intense journey, and found inner peace, I am still longing for a physical, earthly love, and this feeling has not yet left me alone. And I'm ok with that. It's who I am and what makes me, me, and I honour all of it.

This book marks my homecoming; here I finally get to share this part of my story, hoping I can make a positive impact on the world as I leave the past behind for good.

Part 1

Opening the Heart

Chapter 1

Remember Who You Are

❖

At the break of dawn on a brand-new year
I cut the chords to another, when I stepped out of fear.
The weight of desire pulled against me,
lies and deceit unravelled a union that was not meant to be.

Finding solace for my wounded ego
in the comfort of the sisterhood and the odd glass of Prosecco.
Protecting me from my bleeding heart,
women who knew the relationship was doomed from the start.

Blinded by lust and stuck in the story
I lost sight of the truth that others could see.
Questioning how I could let this man into my life,
I had to admit my ego had created this strife.

My relationship with the man I call my ex
reflected something I needed to learn and a lot about sex.
A reflection of my wounded self,
who I called in, so I wouldn't be left on the shelf.

I came to India to find this great love of mine,
but this love is in me, it is the love of the divine.
So, I put pen to paper, my writing healed me,
three books came, forming a trilogy.

The grace of the divine shone deep within me,
she gave me strength to heal the wounds of the patriarchy.
A loveless system of control and divide,
which caused endless suffering to her beloved child.

In this time of rising upon our beautiful Earth,
may we free ourselves from suppression
as a new dawn is birthed.
Let us hold space in circles of twelve,
where into the darkness we must delve.

Releasing the stories of our painful past
into the Heart of Love, free at last.

My journey began after I surrendered to the silence within and connected to the whisper of my soul: sitting in the present, allowing life to reveal itself to me bit by bit. In the sweetness of those moments, I learnt how to be, and found peace inside, walking the way of love, back to self, living a life that I could never have imagined.

But it wasn't always this way.

For years, I pushed and forced and tried my best to control life, squeezing it into a box that I had created inside my mind. I was very rigid in what I believed life should look like. I was a woman driven by ambition and achievement, living the Western dream, wanting all the trappings that went with it. My formulae for life were, to excel at school, get a job, get married, buy a house, have kids and live happily ever after. The end.

Everything I did was focused on achieving that little girl's dream. By my early thirties, I had most of it, although not in a conventional way. I was a single, career mum living on my own, in a beautiful house, one failed relationship down and missing the prized piece of my perfect life puzzle. I still hadn't met my knight in shining armour, whom I believed was the secret to my happiness. And if truth be known I hated the stigma of being a single mum. It made me feel inadequate. I lived in conservative middle-class suburbia and was raised a good Catholic girl, so having children out of wedlock was not congruent with the image of my perfect nuclear family. Horrified by this conditioning, and the feelings I had towards myself, I battled with insecurities, and the lack of compassion I had towards myself, for years. The only time I ever truly felt free of this judgement was when I travelled around India and South East Asia, in my early twenties. None of it seemed to matter then because I was following my heart and was very unattached to anyone or anything. But when I came back to the UK, to 'real' life, I forced myself to conform to society's way again and abandoned myself once more.

After my first relationship failed, I went into a partnership with another man. That lasted two years. The whole thing was a disaster and I only stayed in the relationship because I couldn't bear to be alone. It feels weird to admit it now, but it was the truth at the time. I knew the relationship was wrong from the start, but I was so hell-bent on having family, that I totally compromised myself. The times when I came out of autopilot and caught myself, I questioned what the hell I was doing, but then I went back into autopilot and carried on with the lie. I was totally unaware of the chaos I caused myself and dug myself into a dark hole because I couldn't see how destructive my patterns were and how my lack of self-worth presented in this relationship was not wholesome for me. But one day, something came along that pushed me over the edge, as it always does, and I found the courage to leave. Although it was not easy in the end, endings never are, I will never forget the feelings of relief and sheer joy, to finally be out of that relationship and have my life back again. As joy washed over me, my heart opened and I stopped searching for love and found peace inside. I was relaxed and happy for the first time in years. Two months later my husband walked in. People always say when you stop looking for love, it finds a way to you, and love found me big time. When I met my late husband, we both had that lightning bolt feeling inside and knew instantly that we would spend the rest of our lives together. But our forever only lasted 6 years.

I was widowed at 41, and back searching again.

I spent the next five years grieving, for the life that was taken away before it even really started. I lost faith in everything and was angry with God for doing this to me. As I turned away from God, everything started to fall away. I fought my way through the fog, trying my damndest to hold on to the life I once had, not realising I needed to let go. The first thing to go was my career in the media. After years of working my way up the ranks, I left my job at the BBC, took redundancy, and looked after my baby son who was only 22 months old when his daddy died. I needed a time-out. But instead of taking time for myself, I poured my energy into finishing renovations on my house, which I was in the process of building when my husband died. I went back into autopilot, into doing mode, creating the perfect home, hoping that somehow it would make the pain go away. It didn't.

I then threw myself into yoga and trained as a teacher: still not ready to sit in my pain. I needed to find another way out, and yoga seemed the perfect remedy. The word 'yoga' means to unite. In its purest sense, the practice is designed to unite the mind, body and soul with universal consciousness. In my innocence and desire to help myself and others, I opened my mind up to a vast amount of esoteric knowledge, but most of it was not grounded in experience. Knowledge is not the same as wisdom. We attain wisdom when we experience things in the physical world. Wisdom is lived. Knowledge without experience is just another construct of the mind. My mind ran ahead of itself, leaving my body behind. I became drained and felt empty inside. I had this looming sense that something was about to happen, but I didn't quite know what it was. The day I finally surrendered, was the day I sat in silence for the first time and came off the treadmill of doing. I remember this awful fear and nauseating feeling of nervousness inside of me. I felt like the silence was going to consume me. But as each moment of silence expanded into the next, a space opened up inside of me, and I finally connected to my higher self who guided me to where I am today, one step at a time.

Sitting in stillness and reconnecting to my higher self was like breaking a spell. It was the first step in a long journey home, which I'm still working on, and probably will be for the rest of my life. The journey inward, to find my own truth, instead of turning to others to listen to theirs. You see, until that moment, I couldn't stand in the fire, when I felt something bubbling away inside. I either suppressed the feeling, ignored it, or looked outside myself, to another authority, for answers or the remedy. I never took a moment to stop and ask myself and my body, what it needed. I filled the space inside with distractions from the external world, rather than trusting the wisdom of my internal world. And this wisdom that came from within had the most perfect solution for me; it always does. I just wasn't ready to receive it. Every time I was on the precipice of change, 'outer' distractions would come into my experience and lead me stray. And one of the biggest 'distractions' of all, was my relationship with men, or my 'love' teachers, as I fondly call them.

Over time, I realised my journey, like all our journeys, was designed perfectly for me, by a version of me, that had already walked through to the other side. All I had to do, was get out of my own way and stop trying to control life: allow the path to unfold through me, one step at a time and to relax into life, rather than rushing ahead of myself, second-guessing the next move, which my mind liked to do. As I started to unravel the conscious and unconscious patterns that were running in the background of my life, the way I perceived myself and the world around me, started to change. I had to learn to deal with myself first, which was not always easy. It meant taking full responsibility for my actions, and the pain I caused myself and others, especially when I was so consumed with my own grief and didn't know any better. I wasn't the best mum, in those early days of grieving. I was barely able to look after myself, let alone two kids, and if I'm honest, this left me feeling resentful at times. It took years to reclaim these pent-up emotions and accept myself for my failings at that time. I also had to stop pleasing others, per se. I had this tendency to be super nice and sweet to other people, while sometimes compromising my own needs, which left me feeling resentful and disappointed in myself. Finding myself in compromising situations that didn't resonate with what I truly wanted because I was incapable of speaking my truth, and saying no. Learning to stay open, while maintaining my own ground and integrity was a skill, I am still becoming practiced in. Committing to myself, so that I could trust my inner guidance, knowing that this would help me make better choices, in every aspect of life, including my relationships, was another gift I was nurturing from within. And I had to really take a long hard look at what it is I truly wanted going forward and take action towards achieving it.

Through it all, my greatest challenge was letting go of my childhood dream. For some unbeknown reason, I could not let go of this strong desire to meet someone, get on with my life and be happy. It was like the proverbial thorn in my side and I didn't know why. It wasn't until I moved to India that things started to become clear, as the path ahead spoke to the longing that my heart knew I was destined for. Looking back now I can see how this search for love was my greatest gift and also my worst enemy. I was so invested in finding love, I became a victim in my own play. And yet, all the disappointments, all the broken dreams, actually lead me back to myself and helped me see where I was not being true to myself. It sounds a bit twisted and mixed up, but life can be messy in this way, until we see through the fog, learn to master ourselves and overcome the things that are keeping us down. And my widow story was definitely keeping me down. It was another story on top of all the other stories and labels I had accumulated over the years. All these aspects of me, hidden behind the stories, scattered in the ethers, connected to a fine cord to the ground of luminosity within. The mother, wife, sister, yogi, coffee lover, writer, spiritual badass, media lovie, dancing queen, traveller, thespian and so the list went on. These identities were worn like clothing, piled one on top of each other, as body armour, protecting me from further pain, but in truth, they created more heaviness inside my heart. The more layers I wore, the heavier the burden of weight upon me. To the outside world, I was brave, inspirational even, but inside I was fragile, and clinging to hope, that somehow, I could have my old life back. I grieved for who I thought I was, not realising that she was an empty shell, and the discomfort I was feeling was actually bringing me closer to the new me, the me I am today. It was only when I took off the layers that my need to be validated from the external world disappeared, and I was finally able to reach the core of who I am. I was on the precipice of change, at a crossroads, straddling two worlds: the old and the new. The irony is the times when I thought I was so full of vitality were the times when I avoided myself the most, suppressing the real me as my mind self-censored every move. It was a bit like sitting in darkness at the bottom of a huge hole that I had dug perfectly for myself, not realising I was actually in a hole. Yet all the denial, abandonment of self, and bypassing, were necessary to bring me back to ground zero. My quest for understanding, which took me halfway around the world, was all ultimately designed to bring me back home. The actual physical journey outward eventually brought me inward, back home to the heart. All the yoga, meditation, self-help books and other spiritual practices were tools, to help me along the way. They sustained and helped me, for a while, but I felt like I was scratching at the surface of my being, and sensed there was so much more to discover.

I finally had the space to delve deep into my soul when I moved to Goa, India with my son and settled into a simple life, in nature, surrounded by a community of like-minded people. I spent my days doing all the things I loved: walking on the beach, going to yoga, taking my adorable little boy to school, making new friends and catching up with old friends who came to visit. Monday to Friday, I was a bit of a recluse, writing all day and in my own world, but by Friday I turned into a social butterfly. I was ready for a glass of wine and loved to join the school mums on the beach for a delicious fish curry at one of the local beach huts, while my son played in the sand and splashed in the crystal-clear waters of the Arabian Sea. Life was good, and I finally started to relax into myself again, after the long sadness of the past. I felt a renewed peace and balance inside that I had not known for years. Waking early each morning to write gave me purpose, and filled my heart with joy and promise.

And as I wrote, I slowly awakened inside, to the love that was always there. Connecting to my divinity, opening in faith that everything would align for my highest good. And everything did align divinely, other than this annoying persistent niggle that kept my mind wandering every time I thought about my childlike desire to meet someone. Like destiny calling from the sidelines, never leaving me alone for long. This 'other worldly' feeling was part of me, trying to teach me from within. Yet I had no idea the 'search' was a vital part of the story that was unfolding in me. I felt like I was playing a game of cat and mouse, between my heart and mind. It was a game that was pulling me into the past and taking me out of the present. I later discovered it was all designed to bring me deeper into the truth of who I am and to help me align to this time now on earth. As I was writing, researching and living my life, I was actually being given clues all the time about this ancient biblical story that revealed itself through me in the most surprising of ways. I'll explain more about this later in the book.

It was under a luminous full moon sky
that we cast our magic circle, Jennifer, Alex, Sarah and I.
Sending out letters to the universe,
planting seeds of desire for the dreams that we nursed.

We offered our hearts to the Great Mother above
and held each other tightly in our circle of love.
Together as one in the Arabian Sea,
we watched our letters burn for all eternity.

In faith and in trust the Great Mother did shine
with gifts that showed up in their own divine time.
I watched in awe as my sisters' lives were transformed:
a writer, a healer, a designer was born.

But my heart's desire seemed to elude me,
my impatient soul whispered, "Where are you, my love?
For I cannot see.
This incessant search for 'the one' outside me,
WAS the control of the patriarchy.

Hidden in the depths of my own precious womb
lost to fear and ego, imprisoned by whom?
As he calls from the darkness, "I'm here, my love."
I see the essence of my true nature as below, so above.

Spirit searching for Soul the dance of unity,
together creating the holy trinity.

I started to *observe* myself, in my life, when I connected to the natural world around me. After I dropped my son off at school, I would go for my morning walk along Talpona Beach. At this time in the morning, I was usually the only person on the beach. There would perhaps be a few local fishermen bringing in the morning catch, and some beach dogs hanging around, hoping to get lucky. And of course, the ubiquitous cows which roam freely in Goa as they are revered as sacred to the local Hindu community. There was something about walking barefoot in the sand, with the sun on my skin, and the sound of the ocean all around, that filled my heart with so much joy. I felt my childlike innocence return, and this lightness and freedom allowed my whole being to open up. In this expanded state, I connected to the trees, the ocean, the birds and wildlife all around. It was as if I stepped into a more natural state of being, a state where I was connected to everything, and everything was connected to me. This precious connection to my true self is how nature intended us to be, without the struggles and suffering that we have normalised in life. I was getting a glimpse of how life could be, but first I had to clear out the misunderstanding of the past before I could bring this 'home' state into every waking moment of my life.

I started to actively work on my unseen shadow side when I connected with other women who acted as bright lights for my soul: remarkable women from all over the world. Together we swam through the tides of life, reflecting on the other aspects of self that we could not see in ourselves. In friendship and love, we danced side by side, supporting each other, raising our kids, and doing our best to heal the wounds of the past. It is only when I started to really come back into myself that I could fully appreciate the strength and power of these relationships and the community that welcomed me in and held me tight in Patnem, South Goa where I lived. The expats and locals alike embraced me into their families, and helped me smile again. The local women in the vegetable market brightened up my day, with their infectious laughs when I first arrived and felt lonely and scared. Ibrahim, my beautiful 'fixer' friend, who came to my rescue when I crashed my car into a ditch, more than once! Ibrahim showed up for me when things went wrong, which they did all the time, as I set up home and didn't know what to do. He guided and supported me like I was one of his own. Kisan is the nicest and most trustworthy shop owner in the whole of India, who always had a smile and a patient word for me. Kate, the owner of Jaali Café, which was the epicentre of my social life, was always so helpful and up-to-date on what was happening in the village. Whenever I needed a break from writing, I would head to Jaali and bump into someone for a chat, or hang out with Kate. I was never short of good conversation, and great Wi-Fi which was a rarity in our little piece of South Goa. The families and teachers of River House Academy, where my son attended school, were so generous with their support and friendship to both me and my son. It takes a community to raise a child, a community to live fully, together, for the betterment of all.

As I softened into myself, and dared to see into the unseen, I started to let go of the past and began trusting my own intuition again. I used to stare for hours at an exquisite painting on my bedroom wall called *The Lovers*, an abstract oil canvas of a man and woman energetically entwined as if one. To me, that painting represented everything I was searching for: a beautiful, passionate love and union with a man who was worthy of me. In time, I was to find out that the painting represented much more than just the physical union of a man and woman. It held a hidden message, which I needed to hear. Each morning, during meditation, I would look deep into the heart of that painting wondering what mysteries it was keeping. Sitting in stillness, as stillness itself, the message that came through was very clear. "Dee, you already know. Deep down inside. You already know." In the purity of that moment, I realised I had to go deeper inside myself to understand the mystery that my soul was destined to discover. The echo of the past was calling me in, asking me to face the pain that had been hidden inside of me since the beginning of time. My stomach churned and tears wet my eyes. I was scared of what my heart was asking of me, and my mind wanted none of it. My mind wanted to go back to its 'normal' life, to the safety of the known. It didn't want me to step into this unknown space in the darkness of my being where the gold lay. You see, the painting was showing me something extraordinary that was beyond this world. It was showing me a pathway to peace, which is free of suffering. And this pathway is found inside every single person on Earth. The saying from Hermes Trismegistus, 'as above so below, as within, so without, as the universe, so the soul," is not simply a soundbite, or philosophical phrase, spoken by a wise man in the past. These simple words point to the secret of life itself, which our ancestors knew of, yet we have forgotten. And we receive these ancient wisdoms when the mind is still and the heart is open. The beautiful painting on my wall in Goa was confirming an awareness that was inside of me. It spoke of the holy trinity which is the Sacred Union Within. *When the divine masculine, who reaches to the heavens, and the divine feminine who comes through the Earth, join at the heart, the child of unity is born. Together they bring peace on Earth and a new era of unity for mankind.* 'Man-Kind' will no longer allow its troubles to be played out on each other because we have returned to our true nature, back to 'Kind-Man.' As I gazed into the heart of that painting, I wanted to know what I needed to do, to align with this way of being, and the message I received was: *"You need to reclaim all parts of yourself."* I understood this to mean that I was being asked to heal the trauma of my past, the shadow wounds that were buried in my blood. The lies and betrayal that I was not consciously aware of, which came to me in my relationship with men. These were the wounds of the patriarchy that were hidden deep within my unconscious self, in the memories of abuse and violence inflicted on women throughout the centuries. In the flesh and bones of my body, I was carrying the shame and guilt of many past lives, and these stories were calling to be healed and released into the light.

The more I *observed* myself in my life, the more self-compassion, humbleness and understanding I had for this elusive piece of me that fuelled my quest into the unknown. My desire to meet someone was part of something much bigger than me. It was part of a prophecy that would one day show itself to the world. This dance with my 'love' teachers was ultimately helping me see myself from a new perspective. It allowed me to see the beauty in diversity, and how it is through our differences that we learn and evolve together to create a better world for all: building a society where all are equal; a society where we acknowledge, accept and respect each other's unique journey through life. My relationship with the men in my life, AKA my 'love' teachers, ultimately helped me hold the frequency of love within me so that I could share it with others. As I became more intimate with my own pain and trauma, I developed a huge amount of compassion for what so many people go through, to break free of the limitations of the mind, and eventually heal.

It was through these relationships that I started to take more personal responsibility for my own behaviour. This was challenging at first, as my fragile ego was completely unaware when I was acting out, or suppressing my bullshit. My relationships became containers for deep spiritual growth, although I only developed this awareness years into my journey when I discovered more about my own destiny and purpose. For most of my life, as I said earlier, I had this primal desire to meet someone, settle down and have the happy stable family life that I never had as a kid. I justified this longing because I was born a Gemini, which is the sign of the twins. My brothers are twins, my best friend is a twin and my last partner was a twin. I was surrounded by twins but had no idea what this 'twin' energy signified. All I knew was every relationship I stepped into, blew up in my face, exposing all the trauma and lies inside of me and the other person. When I talked to other women who were on the spiritual path, working on healing themselves, they also experienced a similar thing. Most of the women I met in the conscious communities, were single, because, like me, they found being with a partner extremely challenging. When you are working on healing yourself, and go into a relationship, the trauma inside seems to be magnetised. It takes a very special and committed person to sit in the fire alongside you, as the trauma purges and burns away. Both partners need to be conscious and aware of the process, understanding that the relationship itself is a container for a higher purpose. If one is committed and the other is not, the relationship inevitably ends. Added to this, is the simple fact that there are a lot more women working on themselves than men, so dating someone in the conscious community is a straight-up numbers game. My friend, Jennifer, knew of my frustration and longing, and whenever she did my cards, she spoke of being shown, "two men, with salt and pepper speckled hair." This image of two men was not literal, things rarely are in the spiritual realm. It was a reference to the Twin energy that was coming for me. But in my innocence and ignorance, without being consciously aware I was looking, my mind became slightly curious every time a silver-haired man passed me by on the cosmic highway in Goa. A little voice inside would say, "Is that him, Dee?" It was like this annoying itch that I couldn't scratch, and suddenly there seemed to be grey-haired men absolutely bloody everywhere! All I could see whenever I went out, was silvery grey hair. I used to laugh to myself whenever I walked along Patnem Beach past a silver fox walking the other way. The little voice inside would quietly say, "Maybe that's him, Dee." At other times, I would see a middle-aged guy drive past me on his Enfield bike, looking like an aged hippy, and I'd think, "Please, God, let that not be him!" The truth, though, was that nobody crossed my path or even came close to my heart until 36 hours before I was due to leave Goa to spend the summer back in Europe. The universe chose this moment to literally throw a man at my feet, as if to say, "Well, Dee, if you're so determined to meet someone, then here you go, here's your man." And just for the record, he did have silvery-grey hair!

I speak about this relationship in *Book 2: Dying and the Art of Being*. This man was sent to teach me some very hard lessons that I needed to learn about myself. He shone a spotlight on all the wounds I was holding inside, but could not see: all the lies and betrayals, all the shame and blame; all the trauma from the past that was stuck inside of me came to life through this union and spewed out into my world. Of course, at the time I was unaware of what was happening. I was just a girl looking for love in all the wrong places. Hell-bent on meeting someone, I wove a web of deceit around my heart and tried to make the relationship work, when clearly it couldn't. Our childhood stories came out to play, like two kids playing doctors and nurses. I projected on him; he acted it out. As I loved bombed him with excessive compliments and kindness, he behaved in a very dishonourable manner. Unable to express my true feelings when things played out, I swallowed the pain inside and kept myself locked in chains, as the bondage of trauma, which brought us together, grew stronger. At the time I didn't have the tools to deal with my strong feelings in a calm and peaceful way, as they rose inside me. These strong surges in feelings or emotions are designed to move you. We are meant to purge our feelings because we are not designed to hold on to them. But if we get them out of ourselves, in a destructive way, by dumping them on someone else, we just perpetuate more chaos in the world.

When I was in this relationship, I couldn't see through the fog that was clouding each moment. So, my pain and suffering were driven deeper inside of me, waiting for another opportunity to be seen. The divine child in me was trapped beyond the darkness in my heart, and I longed to reach her. She was hidden behind the veil. Every bit of pain, humiliation, disappointment, lies, jealousy and betrayal that I had ever created was preventing me from reaching her. Although my relationship with my ex was fraught with tribulation, it helped me realise the depths I needed to go to, to heal my childhood trauma. For that alone, I will always be truly grateful for the experience, even though it was not easy at the time. And I also learnt that I did not want to pass my stuff onto another person, harming myself and the other in the process.

***

We perceive the world through 5 planes of reality: the emotional plane is the energy that runs and moves you; the physical reality is how you relate to the world through your body; the spiritual plane is the understanding that something greater than you is at play; the virtual reality is your imagination; the mental plane is the clarity of thought, which improves when all four planes are in balance. When this happens, you can perceive yourself in the world with a lot more love and compassion, for all that life is. When the planes are balanced, we tend not to be hard on ourselves, or overly self-critical if something goes wrong, rather we objectively move through life, learning from our mistakes with grace and ease, making the necessary changes so that we do not make the same mistake again. Imagine the 4 planes form the axis of a cross, and you are at the heart of your own individual cross. How you translate reality, in your day-to-day life, depends on how finely tuned and balanced these 4 quadrants of reality are. The place where pure love resides is at the heart of the cross, where all 4 realities meet, in perfect balance and harmony. Every time we meet ourselves here, we create from pure love, as nature intended. The problem is we've forgotten what this home state feels like. You see, the moment we step out of the womb, we are subject to someone else's viewpoint, and this conditioning clouds our sense of reality. In our innocence, we believe what the outside world tells us, often empowering these viewpoints rather than listening to our own, innate intelligence that comes from within. Firstly, we turn to our parents for our basic needs and survival. Then, we are influenced by our schooling system, and religion, as we look to our teachers and clergy for educational and spiritual guidance. When we grow into our teens, we seek validation from our peer group for our emotional well-being. We turn to the medical system for our physical health. And look to our governments, and financial systems to organise and manage us. We give all of our power and authority away to these entities outside ourselves, not realising that it affects the purity of our connection to our own source of creation, and this in turn affects how we translate reality. For example, I grew up Roman Catholic to working-class Irish immigrants and took on the persona of the 'good' girl in my family. So, my upbringing affected how I perceived what was right and wrong in my world, and this, in turn, influenced my relationship with money, with authority, with sexuality, with my body, with people pleasing, and eventually with God. This sent me on a downward spiral of bulimia and poor self-esteem and, as I denied many aspects of myself, I ended up hating my body and being frightened of life. What happened then, is I locked these aspects of myself away and denied myself. At times, I overcompensated and went into addictive behaviours, over-exercising, drinking too much, starving my body, or overfeeding my suppressed sexual desire which could not be quenched. At other times, I went the opposite way and completely suppressed my desires, cutting myself off from the basic pleasures in life, and hiding myself away. I yoyoed from one extreme to another, totally out of balance with life itself. And consequently, most of my relationships were with men who were similarly out of balance. By not being present in myself, it was almost impossible to reach out to another person and to love them in a whole and honest way, as me. Because the truth was, I had no idea who I was.

So, finding balance became my priority. As I took a long hard look at myself, I saw how I had stepped into the role of the 'strong' female, which left very little space for an actual man to be present in my life. My past relationship was such a gift because it gave me a huge wake-up call to integrate and connect deeper to myself, and to own my vulnerability. I had to witness where I was still holding onto the stories, that had been recycling through me for aeons, that spoke to a lack of self-worth and fear. And that was not easy. As I sat with myself, in silence, I saw an image of a little girl, curled up into a ball, dreaming of her knight in shining armour. *This belief that I could be saved by another, became the fabric of my life, and the source of my separation from self.* And this belief that someone outside of self can give you love, was perpetuated by the world around me. From most of my childhood fairy tales to the blockbuster chick flicks I adored, to the folklores, legends and prophecies I read about in my spiritual quest for understanding and answers. There was no escaping this so-called 'happy ever after' that seemed to rub salt in the wound as I journeyed through the labyrinth of life. It was only when I sat with myself, in the silence once again, that I began to see how the story itself is a metaphor for my own self-realisation. The dragon self is this pure force of nature within every person, that when activated slays the egotistic programmes of the lower mind, to rescue the 'damsel in distress', which is the divine child. This divine child is the unity of our nature that sits at the heart of the cross, in a space of pure love where creation resides. As I came down from the cross and looked at myself in the mirror, I saw a complex multi-dimensional being reflected back at me, with many attributes and facets that make me whole and complete.

She is The Lover that everyone knows,
for her love is the light, her love is the Rose.
She is The Alchemist connected to her power,
a pure divine medicine that will never turn sour.

She is The Moon that comes out at night,
nourishing the waters so she can take flight.
She is The Observer, presence in service,
burning old memories in her fiery furnace.

She is The Fairy Godmother, a being of light,
a woman by day, an angel by night.
She is The Child with big bright eyes,
she feels the pain of others that they try to disguise.

She is The Crone, an intuitive sage,
for her teachings are magical and get better with age.
She is The Illumined One who ignites the purple flame,
for her love is a gift, her love transmutes shame.

She is The Queen protective of her tribe,
if you get on her wrong side, you'll rattle her vibe.
She is The Warrior fighting for the Just,
betrayed by those she thought she could trust.

She is The Goddess, graceful and wise,
for her love is compassion that shines through her eyes.
She is The Mother, the giver of life,
the protector, the destroyer and the Divine Wife.

As I connected to my multi-dimensional self, different parts of my being started to reveal themselves to me. Aspects of the soul that I had forgotten about, that needed to be reclaimed and integrated to restore wholeness, were bringing me closer to my divine blueprint, as my DNA awakened inside of me. My soul was on a voyage to retrieve all parts of herself, and to bring them back into the heart of love. I use the concept of '12 around 1' as a metaphor to help me remember my *original* Galactic Origins. The memory of this was brought back to Earth over 2000 years ago by Yeshua, or Jesus Christ, who embodied the full Kristos template, bringing it into the Earth grid to help humanity awaken once again, after the fall. We tend to write Kristos with a CH so Christos, which is why Yeshua is known as Jesus - The Christ, which is a reference to the energy he embodied. This Grand Awakening that has been prophesied for centuries, is happening now on Earth, and you and I have ring-side seats. The fall of man, as is talked about in the Bible, and in many other scriptures, is the disconnection from our true blueprint and God source consciousness. The complexities of the Cosmos, and ourselves as beings of light, are way vaster than we could ever imagine, and we only start to remember who we are once we reconnect to God source consciousness again. As we do this, the primal masculine and feminine energy of God source consciousness flows throughout all the universes, and our bodies, and this is how we evolve. Influxes of high-frequency plasma light are creating a bio-spiritual re-genesis throughout our universe and, as it does, our DNA collects more and more energetic frequency within its strands. In doing so, it helps prepare the physical body to hold more and more dimensional frequency. Our DNA is aligned with our consciousness. The more DNA we have assembled, as per our lighted design, the higher and more aware our consciousness becomes. This consciousness helps us understand the structure of universal existence from the density of the material world here on Earth, to the workings of plasma light in the cosmos, and beyond into the heavens and the world of antimatter. The Kristos template teaches you about the Way of Love, and this template is held inside our bodies. As within, so without. Love as a frequency is the most powerful resource in the entire universe, and when we connect to the 12th-dimensional aspect, of God source consciousness, we naturally activate the inner technology inside our bodies, and one by one, we walk our way home, as we are restored to our divine angelic selves.

Much may be written in the future about the Galactic Wars that took place for aeons to bring us to this moment: about the malevolent forces at play, that tried everything in their power to prevent this awakening from occurring. What's been going on behind the scenes, and which many Hollywood blockbusters, like the Star Wars films, have alluded to, is mindboggling to say the least. But if truth be known, the fall, of man, happens every moment we choose fear over love. Every time we get involved in thinking or actions, where we become a victim or victimiser, when we get enmeshed in stories of shame and blame, force and fear, we fall from freedom and trap ourselves inside the matrix of the mind. And we get sucked back into the pain and struggles, and energetic forces, that have been controlling many descending universes for aeons. The Kristos way teaches you to find stillness through the way of 'atonement' or *at-one-ment*. When you come into presence, at the heart of your being, in the oneness of the moment, your connection to universal God source consciousness, purifies you, one moment at a time. Everyone on Earth is at a different stage in their own personal evolution, as well as being connected to the collective evolution of humanity. Those who are out in front, bringing through energies of God Source consciousness to the planet, laying the foundations for New

Earth that is being created, have been tirelessly, and quietly, working in the background to pave the way for others. When we turn away from God source consciousness, we cannot connect to the eternal natural flow of source energy, so we have to consume energy from other sources, outside ourselves, that gets recycled throughout the lower frequencies of the descending universes. That's why, despite all the years of working on ourselves, we have constantly looped around the same issues, stories and struggles that affect our lives. Our Earth too has been cut off from the main primal source of fresh revitalising energy. She too has been in a perpetual cycle of death and decay, until now. This separation from source energy is what causes the pain and suffering in our world. It's why we act in ways that go against our true nature. The grief and loss we feel on a deep cellular level because of this separation from source energy is what causes disease in our body, and ageing. As more and more people connect to God Source Consciousness, their DNA is activated, and the cells in our bodies start to awaken. Our mind switches off from harmful thoughts, and the body starts to regenerate naturally. Our being is already multi-dimensional and exists in higher planes of reality, we just have to match our bodies' consciousness to meet it. And we can only access this inside ourselves. When we feel expanded, calm and peaceful, then we are in resonance with this higher state of being. When we feel contracted, discomfort and fearful, then we are out of alignment with this higher state of being.

Discernment is the ability to feel the truth inside our body, beyond what words are said. Until we step out of the past, we are locked in a cycle of creation from the memories of who we used to be. As our consciousness evolves, it pulls us into memories of the past, to collapse them, so that we no longer create from a past version of ourselves. When this happens, we feel a bit untethered, like we're losing our minds, and in truth, we are. But as we dissolve the memories, we also dissolve the pain patterns and all associations to the past. When you bring a higher version of yourself into the now, you move between different realities all the time. Some people call this time travel, but you're not actually going anywhere, rather these memories of the past, future and parallel lives, are all unfolding inside of you, through you, in the now, as your consciousness moves from one place to another. It's quite a ride! When you are in the eternal now, your soul reveals itself to you organically, as you live your life, in the moment, one step at a time. These different streams of consciousness flow through you all the time, oscillating at different vibrations, so we rarely stay at one octave of reality. We constantly shift, move and change as we learn mastery of ourselves. This self-mastery helps and guides us to thoughts, actions and behaviours that lead to higher and higher paths. The problem is we've all been programmed to believe that we have to suffer in life, so we expect to experience suffering in everyday life. But suffering is an old belief, and we are all capable of breaking free of this thinking. We do not need to suffer in the name of love. If you are reading this book now, you have the potential to break free of suffering, to free your mind, and to bring all your potential into this one moment: now, where there is no place for suffering, there is only love. In the timeless now, your mind doesn't dictate who you are. You gain all the memories of your past, and all the futures, and realise you are the totality of all that you are. You are everything, everywhere, all at once, and it is from this place that you experience true freedom, and create from it. Reality is not linear, so you can be all things at once, which makes life truly expansive, and very, very interesting!

Sweet beloved Rose, Sisterhood of divine,
enlightened beings in your heart and mine.
High Priestesses on earth they shared their essence,
now rays of light for the 'I Am' presence.
In circles of love, they gather magically,
to activate the flame in the heart of humanity.

Twin men and women together as one,
hold secrets to the path of our ascension.

Their light driven underground throughout the dark ages,
barely flickering from fear, but still courageous.
Protected for aeons by the Council of Light,
this is the flame God needs to ignite.

God and Goddess return through the Christ Consciousness,
remember your connection to divine oneness.

Chapter 2

Why Did God Make Me?

❖

As I sat down one day with my curious child,
he asked a question as Spirit smiled:
"Mummy, why do you think God made me,
if God is perfect as perfect can be?"

Philosophers and wise men throughout history
have spent aeons pondering this great mystery.
If God is all that is seen and unseen,
then this love is in everything that has ever been.

"Well, if that is the case," my little one replied:
"Then God must be in everything, and everything is I."
"'Tis true dear one, God is everything below and above,
God is All, God is love."

Earth was created as a cosmic experiment,
out of curiosity and for God's merriment.
Our purpose on Earth is to love without remorse,
and to bring this wisdom back to source.

But we've taken this gift from the universe,
stripped her bare and made her worse.
My son looked at me with a mischievous smile,
as he pondered this predicament for a while.

"I'm not so sure, Mummy, I think God's plan was flawed,
I don't think God was curious, I think he was bored!"

You are connected to life in all that is seen and unseen. The unseen world is infinite in nature and speaks to you through your soul. If you look at life through a philosophical lens, then you might say you come to Earth to learn and evolve. If you imagine Earth is like a gigantic soul school, then you have to pass certain lessons before you can ascend to higher ground. Yet this gigantic soul school on Earth has some very funny rules. We all have the free will to ignore the natural laws of the universe and act without restraint. You can if you like, do as you please, but this tends to get you into a whole lot of trouble! Secondly, when you come to Earth, you are born with no memory of who you are and why you are here ... it really is a crazy mind game if you think about it! Before your soul is birthed into your body, you review your past life lessons and your previous experiences on Earth, as you are shown your book of life in the afterlife (I talk all about this in book two, *Dying and the Art of Being*). You get to see all the lessons you've mastered and tick them off and you get to review the lessons you still need to understand. Then you make a contract to return once again, into a new life, to repeat the lessons you hadn't learnt from your previous experience on this planet. But here's the twist: when you're born, your memory bank is erased and you don't know why you are here and what these lessons are. It seems as if the system is flawed, or else whoever is in charge 'up there' has a very good sense of humour! You might question why a loving, generous, patient and kind creator would do this to you. Why would we come to Earth and make life so difficult for ourselves? The answer is that there is a lot of wisdom to be earned in learning our lessons, and when you share that wisdom with those around you and eventually bring it back to its source, into your hearts, it can be used to create more love, and so, we evolve as a planet and a civilisation. And, that's exactly what is happening now on Earth. Some people are pioneering The Way of Love, who have managed to transcend the death realms and therefore can see beyond the veil and complete their contracts. They are turning the misunderstandings of their lives into more love. Because of this, they are able to anchor more light into their bodies and the Earth, and this Celestial light is helping the Earth purify, and everyone on it. This remarkable feat in human evolution means that humanity can achieve higher levels of spiritual maturity inside our bodies, without passing over. And we can achieve this awareness consciously. In time, this awareness will help us act in kinder, more thoughtful ways, and in turn, we will evolve into a race of people who are more conscious of our behaviour towards ourselves, the planet and others. Nonetheless, some of you are a little stubborn, and not so willing to learn, so you get caught up in patterns of behaviour where you attract the same thing over and over again, and it becomes a bit like *Groundhog Day*. But the lessons don't get any easier; they get harder and harder as your souls silently screech, "For the love of God, have you not worked it out yet?" This goes on until the universe unfortunately has to dish out a drastic life event to wake you up and force you into action.

The great philosophy of Buddhism and the laws of Hinduism taught us this wisdom through the wheel of karma. You clear your karmic debt in this life by learning to have love and compassion for all things. You do this by understanding that *you are connected to everything and every experience is created through your mind.* Your soul takes you into experiences to help clear this Karmic debt. It used to take years and many lifetimes to clear karma, but that phase for humanity is over. You are now living in an era where the realm of cause and effect is playing out on Earth, so your actions can be seen in real-time, almost instantaneously. This means that you are able to create and clear your own path in the moment. To do this you need to achieve a level of self-mastery in yourself, to be able to witness your behaviours playing out in the world. This self-mastery can be achieved very simply if you connect to yourself in silence for as little as five minutes a day. When you relax into your body, and allow the process to occur, nature will purify you without you doing anything. You just need to receive the gift of this time. When you connect in this way, you absorb pure love from nothing into the physical, emotional, spiritual and mental bodies, building up a charge inside of you. Over time, this charge gets stronger and you feel the fire of your intelligence, your innate wisdom activating and flowing through everything.

I searched for answers deep in me
as I walked the path to mastery.
Feeling deep stirrings within,
calling me deeper into my origins.

Profound teachings were revealed,
gifted to me so I could be healed.
Wisdom from philosophy, science and spirituality,
three pillars of Truth for the world we can see.

Everything in life is connected to force,
it's in each and every one of us and is called source.
We weave our unique stories in time,
as earthly and cosmic expressions of thine.

The scientists, philosophers and theologians agree
this source is so powerful it must remain mystery.
We relate to it with our higher heart and mind,
through self-love which we must find.

The mystery is the key to all understanding,
acceptance of this can be very demanding.
The unknown reveals itself in her own special way,
the timing for which I cannot say.

The moment I think I know what's happening,
the mystery loses its meaning.
Life's constant challenge is to awaken to essence,
taught to us through the 'I Am' presence.

All that was born and was ever created
goes back to the source after being separated.
So, everything we see around us has
consciousness and is divine,
the whole world is our creation yours and mine.

Our ancestors spoke of the energy that connects our earthly bodies to the cosmos through the metaphor of the Tree of Life. Images depicting the Tree of Life, traditionally show seven branches pointing upwards to the heavens, representing our connection to the cosmos, and stars. And seven roots pointing downwards to the Earth, representing our connection to our planet, the elements of the material world, and the plant and animal kingdoms. Every man, woman and child has their place at the centre of their own unique Tree of Life, between worlds and between the forces of the cosmos and the heavens and the forces of the Earth and the terrestrial world. Your roots connect you to the forces of Mother Earth and the five elements: earth, fire, water, air and metal, and to earthly life itself. Your branches connect you to the cosmic powers of the Heavenly Father and the forces of eternal life, love, power, peace, wisdom and creativity. The Tree of Life as a metaphor, teaches us that to be in perfect harmony and balance in this life, we need to be centred and aligned to all the forces around us: the spiritual, mental, emotional, virtual and physical forces of our being. When we are rooted in the earth and allow Mother Earth's consciousness to meet the heavenly cosmic forces at the heart, we receive, absorb and transmit pure love, and everyone under our branches and in our radius is strengthened by this presence.

The position of the body at the centre of the Tree of Life also corresponds with the position of our organs. The lower half of the body – the organs of the gastric and reproductive systems – belong to the earthly forces and are the instruments of self-preservation and self-perpetuation. These remain locked in habit patterns and conditioning until we break free of our unconscious behaviours and work in harmony with our body's needs. The upper half of the body – the lungs and the brain – belong to the heavenly forces and are the instruments of breath and thought that belong to the finer forces of the universe. When we learn to connect with the forces of nature, in a practical sense during our everyday activities, we step into our power and can access our highest potential, radically changing and transforming our lives forever. To do this, we have to learn to ride the waves of change, letting go of our past and our fears and trusting these forces within to guide us. The number seven denotes the main chakras, which form a central column of light, which receives a universal current filling the body with pure love. Your body receives and transmits signals into the universe, which is your own personal soul signature. When you start to accelerate in frequency, you get to a point of expansion, where a reversal happens inside of you, and it feels like you start to bring everything back into your physical body. This reclaiming of all that you are, starts to self-heal and purify the body, by pushing up everything that is leaving from the lower density, inside of you, as you rise higher and higher into the stars. You are no longer stuck in descended realities; you are now ascending to higher planes of reality.

Mother Earth, a living, breathing entity,
like us she is changing, we must face this reality.
Our DNA evolves when we raise consciousness,
this paradigm shift to New Earth will bring us into oneness.

When we ascend to higher levels of frequency,
we experience constant changes in the body.
Observing this for the past seven years,
the symptom I experience the most is ringing in my ears.

As Gateways to my inner self open,
I finally realise I'm not mad or broken!
More alive and vital than ever before,
my heart is the gateway to the divine door.

My body is lighter, from natural nutrition
that helps me fly high and achieve my soul mission.
My process of change is well underway,
healing the body to keep disease at bay.

When we take responsibility for our own reality,
we have to drop stories of negativity.
May you surrender to your divinity,
spirit and soul together as one not separately.

Now is the time in our history,
to awaken to a new paradigm and live in harmony.

As the soul of the planet evolves and changes, each person on Earth has an important choice to make. You either evolve and shift into the new Earth or you exit with the old. Ultimately, the decision is made at a soul level, based on the experiences needed for the individual's evolution. There is no right or wrong decision. Every choice is perfect for that individual's lighted design. Those people who exit, do so because they have more to learn through the old way of life, so they reincarnate again and start their soul journey in a new body as life on Earth, or elsewhere, depending on what their soul needs. Those who stay, help build a new world, where there are infinite possibilities, to create life in a peaceful and harmonious way. This time of great change and transition on Earth is very unsettling, especially for those who have not yet awakened to the changes that are occurring throughout the cosmos.

Everything we have ever known is about to change and this can be frightening, for many. So, those who are a little ahead of the game, need to be kind and compassionate to those who are experiencing a shift inside. The most helpful thing to do right now is to live authentically, in the very best way you can, and not be influenced by others or try to interfere with other people's lives. And, as you honour the path of others, and this rule of non-interference, you learn to accept that it is not your job to change, fix, or hang onto people who do not serve the one higher purpose. People who are not meant to be in your world simply won't stick around as you shift and evolve – and that's OK. As you start to purify, you push up against everything that is leaving your field from the old world, which can be very challenging to observe. You will bump up against situations that appal you, such as betrayal, lies, or violence. But you understand very quickly that these experiences are not you. They are leaving, and you need to allow the process to occur. You have to observe it, not touch it. There is nothing for you to do, nothing for you to resolve, you just have to relax, and allow it to be. From here, you start to create your own reality by BEING the best you can in this world. As you evolve, you start to shift in and out of different dimensions the whole time and begin to notice how people move in and out of your lives as they no longer resonate on your wavelength. It's like a gradual clearing-out process that is happening behind the scenes without you realising it. All you can do is focus on your world as it is now. You have to let go of the idea of karma as none of it matters. You need to learn the lessons, as they present themselves in the moment, forgive, let go and move on. And you have to stop fearing what is in front of you because this fear holds you down, and doesn't help you move forward. Each time you fear something, you give energy and feed what you don't want; you have to start to learn to trust. Fear is the story that binds you to the past. Once you let it go, you can light the way for others to join you in the thousand years of peace that has been predicted on this New Earth.

When you start to unravel from the old world, you enter a process of clearing out everything that no longer resonates with the higher version of yourself that you are birthing from within. This means everything in your life that you previously held to be true, you may no longer believe in. This natural evolution of self can be very destabilising and upsetting at times. You can feel like you've been lied to and misinformed about many aspects of life and it's hard to not want to lash out and vilify others for their part in your evolution. It can also feel like your life is falling apart, that you're somehow losing your mind, and in many ways, you are, because the programmes that sit in your mind are being dismantled one by one. This is a time for great acceptance and kindness towards yourself and others while understanding that something greater is at play and that you only have a tiny piece of the picture at any given time. Your relationship with work, money, food, family, friends, your body, the government, the health system, education and religion – it all radically changes. Your relationship with religion or spirituality is the last thing to change because this is fundamental to your understanding of God, and the nature of reality itself.

When my own purification started, I can honestly say I thought I was going mad. Many weird and wonderful things happened during the first few years of clearing as my mind went into overdrive trying to analyse and understand everything. The energy took me into stories of past lives, parallel lives, and multiple lives all at once – it was pretty wild. As my system was being purged, I connected to and balanced the forces within me that awakened my consciousness and helped me understand the deeper truths connected to this time on Earth and our Galactic heritage. When I started this journey, as I said in the introduction, there were very few people I could speak to, and I realise now, I went through this upgrade early, so I could help others, for the time is coming when the rest of humanity goes through this Great Awakening.

One of the hardest things I had to learn was to stop giving meaning to everything that was happening to me, and just allow it to pass on by. Unbeknown to me, every time I gave meaning to something, I was energetically holding on and re-energising the situation that triggered the experience and the programme that was calling to be cleared. I knew I needed to be alert to the divine signalling, but my job was to observe and let go, observe and let go, observe and let go. I soon learnt that my power came from the little micro-decisions I made in every moment, the behind-the-scenes events as I like to call them. The things that others never see are what really count. Every time I smile at a stranger or stare up at the stars, or listen to the birds, or water the plants, every footstep, every whisper into the unknown, it all counts. I started to explore my highest potential by self-mastering unconditional love for myself, through my relationship with others. I could literally see parts of myself in them and recognise my own need to turn inward every time something piqued my attention. As my soul evolved, and continues to evolve, I became aligned to the octave of frequency from the Galactic Centre that is way beyond what I have ever known. I kept magnetising situations and experiences, to fill the void, this black hole inside of me, until I finally realised that I couldn't externalise the need for love; I had to find the source of infinite love inside of me. I had what I affectionately called my, 'it's all me, black hole moment', where my consciousness literally fell into itself, and I rebirthed out the other side. Once this happened, everything shifted and I started the process of embodying the experience so that I could share the wisdom in this book, to help others understand the importance of mastering the relationship with Self, and others.

When I started to heal my relationship with myself, I made new connections with people around me that were less needy or toxic. There were fewer dramas in my life and fewer moments when I doubted myself and questioned what the hell I was doing. I noticed I didn't hold unpleasant feelings inside anymore, I had finally developed an efficiency in letting go. I didn't have to get into endless fights or defend my way of life to others who perhaps had a different viewpoint because the power in me spoke way louder than any words ever could. I had far fewer conversations where the true meaning of what was being said was lost in translation. I could sense when someone was lying and when someone was being truthful. In fact, people seemed to be incapable of not speaking their truth because I had finally learnt to speak mine. People also started opening up to me, telling me secrets that they had held onto for years, knowing that I would hold their confidence and not judge them. I also started to connect to much higher octave Beings who are tapped into their own source connection, and these relationships became a brand-new platform for growth and sharing. I learnt about quantum fields and technology that was quite literally out of this world, and way above what I could imagine possible on Earth. I sat with a group of amazing souls for two years as we fast-tracked through soul school, learning how to navigate these times so that we could help others. As the drama unfolded on the world stage, I knew I would be called to sit in divine neutrality, to be there for friends and family and to help when the old world starts to dismantle around us.

One of the hardest struggles I had when I went through my own unravelling was the untangling of my religious beliefs that I had adopted from my Catholic upbringing. The fight to reclaim my own personal connection with God was profound, and scary at times.

When I lived in India, I kept bumping up against the story of Jesus, the disciples and Mary Magdalene in the divine signals in my reality, but I had no idea what the story was trying to teach me. It was very confusing and spun me around, as it tried to show me the depths of my programming, and the influence that my Roman Catholic upbringing had on my psyche. But as I shifted and awakened inside, I began to break free of the beliefs that kept my heart in chains as I followed my own path of self-enquiry which came from within. There were many times, when I felt very split and separated from the innocence of my true nature, as if I were in two worlds, and the pull to the old was very strong. Unbeknown to me, I was holding onto so much fear. But as more of my true nature came online, the more connected I felt to my truth within, and this restored my faith and helped me face the biggest fears within me. This imbalance inside of me, was being played out in the world outside of me. As my mind ran the show, I unconsciously analysed and judged myself through a distorted lens that was highly critical, and prone to perfectionism. There was a war blazing inside of me, between my mind and heart, between the old way of doing things and the new. I call the old way the 'masculine' thinking way: the way of power over, the way of control, the way of the known. The way of elevating oneself to a higher power and status outside of self. It is the outside-in approach to life: it is a way of validating the self, based on everything on the outside that we as humanity have been trained to do for the past 200 years. And much to my horror, I saw how I held myself accountable based on how I looked, and my lifestyle, as opposed to how I was 'genuinely' feeling inside. The new way which leads you to freedom, and higher states of consciousness is the inside-out approach. It's the way of the *feminine feeling heart*. It's the way of *feelings*, experience, intuition and love. This is the way of stillness, connection and presence in *every aspect of life*. It's a way that allows for life to flow, without the brainwashing of the mind. This requires that you let go of all the confines of what you believe to be right and wrong from the old way of doing things, not just in mediation, or a yoga class, but in everything you do. It's a way of being in everyday life, that calls for comfort in the unknown and allows for spontaneity to lead the way. There is no force behind this way, yet it requires action, and a willingness to sit in your own fire as you burn through all the dross and memories of the past. And action in connecting to yourself every day, which as I said before, can be as little as five minutes at the start of each day. When I speak of the feminine-feeling heart, I am not speaking about gender. People often confuse the concept of 'feminine' with females, and 'masculine' with males, but energy itself is neutral. Energy just is. *When I refer to the Mother or Divine Feminine, I'm referring to the earthy connection to the self, inside the body. When I refer to the Father or Divine Masculine, I'm referring to your Galactic connection, to the heavens, that you bring into the body. And the two become one in the heart.* This is how you bring heaven to Earth.

How you connect to God inside your body. And this is what the story of Yeshua and Mary Magdalene was calling me to remember.

Our ancestors knew of the principles of nature, and referred to their powers in many ways, by leaving us myths, legends, symbols, and stories so that their wisdom was not lost in time. The Ancient Egyptians spoke of these powers through the Goddess Isis, who they referred to as 'I AM' Presence of the Divine Mother. To discover the mysteries of the Divine in the ancient world was to discover the mystery of life itself. Initiates knew this as, "Pulling back the veil of Isis." Isis was one of only a handful of Goddesses considered to be both a solar and lunar Goddess. In other words, she was seen as having both masculine and feminine aspects in perfect balance. The path of mastery to enlightenment, which was taught throughout the mystery schools, was known as The Middle Way. The veil of Isis is a metaphor for the covering of the divine or the unseen. It teaches us that it is hard to see what is not there, but just because we can't see it doesn't mean it doesn't exist. The veil is connected to the principles of nature, the 5 elements and all living things. Everything in the universe is made up of the same fundamental building blocks, which turn energy into matter. Scientists refer to these building blocks as the Vector Equilibrium, or VE. One cannot observe the VE in the material world because it is the geometry of absolute balance. And when there is Absolute balance, there is nothing. No form. A void. Our physical life is created from moment to moment, from this space of nothingness, from this void, and we connect to it through the heart. The VE forms primary patterns known as the Torus, and these shapes are seen everywhere at a micro and macro level: in every atom and cell in plants, animals and humans, and the cosmos as a whole. The Torus is the only geometric form where all forces are equal and balanced. The Torus is dynamic and can sustain itself from the same substance as its surroundings, just like a tornado, a smoke ring in the air, or a whirlpool in the water. And we live in the centre of our own Toroidal field. There are electromagnetic fields around everyone on Earth. They are distinct to each of us, but connected to the universe as a whole. The axis of the Torus extends from the heart down to the pelvic floor, or first chakra into the earth grid, and up to the top of the head, or crown chakra. But a further five chakras outside the body connect us to the cosmos. It is through these subtle energy channels that our masculine and feminine energies join together to send energy up through the chakras to create the field around the body, which is how we connect to the world around us. Ultimately, we experience life on Earth as waves of energy, expanding and contracting as moments in time, which unfold from the cosmos, and return to it. We create the world around us from our own personal energy field. When we connect to our light within, we start the process of embodying our energic field. This calls us back into balance, bringing us into harmony, and connecting us with our divine blueprint as nature intended. I learnt about this pathway back to self via the teachings of the Kristos template that slowly activated inside of me and called my back into stories of the past so that I could reclaim my power and purify within. The veil represents the mystery of life itself; the divinity that connects everyone to everything. Yet this mystery has been lost in the illusion of separation and duality. This started some 7000 years ago, with the spread of patriarchal societies, which occurred as people became more mobile and started to fight for land and power. These intensified in the teachings of the Abrahamic religions, which presented the mystery of life as the duality of heaven and hell. As the God Head is Masculine only, when in fact the God Head has both Masculine and Feminine aspects. In Abrahamic religions, God is seen as the omnipotent, omnipresent creator of the universe: the Heavenly Father who resides up above in the skies. He is transcendent – outside of the self and outside of space and time – and therefore *not within creation* itself. Notwithstanding, he is also a personal God who listens to prayers and reacts to the actions of his subjects. Those who embrace God's love and his word will be joined again with the Father in heaven. And those who don't, will return to hell down below, which is a place of torment and punishment. As a child, the notion of a punishing God scared the bloody life out of me. I was constantly terrified of doing wrong, worried that God might find out. This fear became locked inside my psyche and cast a dark shadow on my life. I took on the persona of the 'good girl', and suppressed aspects of myself that I deemed to be 'not good'. It took years of shadow work to unravel all the guilt, shame, anger, desire and fear from this time, and a huge amount of courage to step beyond this belief and experience *creation from within*. How we understand ourselves and life is personal to each individual, and I respect those who find comfort and strength from their religious beliefs. But I no longer felt this way, and as I searched for truth deep within my heart, this notion of a God separate from self, became a great catalyst for change. The idea of a monolithic God just didn't sit well with me. So, I searched for answers, not really knowing that the search itself was a potent force that would bring me back to my true nature. It first called me outside of myself, into the world, as I journeyed across India, Ibiza, France and Bali, visiting sacred sites, learning from the lands, her peoples and the animal and plant kingdom. Then I was called back into myself, only to find I had the answer inside all along. Once I became self-realised in this way, which took about 2 years of quiet, alone time and self-enquiry, while I lived in Bali, I was able to go back out into the world with this new state of awareness. I liken this to coming home or coming full circle. My path actually led me back to the UK, to my country of birth, where I noticed that everything had changed, yet nothing had changed. Rather it was my perception of reality that had massively shifted from this new higher state of consciousness. I parted the veils to the unseen, and the unknown, and connected to my own divinity within. This connection to Mother Earth Consciousness is an energetic experience that purifies the body, bringing on a physical transformation. The pathway to our divinity is found between the left and right hemispheres of the brain. We have what is known as a tri-nervous system, which is made up of the sympathetic, parasympathetic and central nervous systems. This correlates to the three energy channels in Indian medicine and spiritual science; the Ida is the female left side, the Pingala is the right male side and the Sushumna is the central channel for the Kundalini -Mother Earth energy to rise. The parasympathetic and the sympathetic nervous systems must be activated and work in perfect balance to send Mother Earth's energy up to the central nervous system and awaken the light within us. In Egyptian Mythology, these forces are represented symbolically by Isis and Osiris, through their story of rebirth and renewal. In fact, many ancient stories, including that of Jesus and Mary Magdalene - which I will go on to explore in Part 3, teach us how to activate higher states of consciousness. We do this by overcoming our demons, aka fears, and reclaiming the parts of ourselves, that we lost in the wilderness, to things outside ourselves, when we gave our power away. Once we awaken our divinity within, we reclaim this power and return to our original wholeness. To come into alignment, we have to balance the forces of nature. We do this by observing ourselves in the world and making changes in the inner landscape of our being. When we are too yang and have too much masculine energy, we may be controlling and aggressive, not allowing life to flow through us with ease. When these characteristics present, we tend to hold onto the past. When we are too yin and have too much feminine energy, we are passive and not motivated to connect to our reality. We tend not to take action when action is needed. This energy can leave us a bit scattered, and indecisive and we may miss opportunities when they present themselves. When we come into alignment, we awaken our third eye and gain access to a more neutral, higher state of consciousness, which comes with gifts of inner sight, inner sound and inner knowing. When the forces of nature are balanced, an energetic alignment occurs which is known as the Sacred Union. This union happens *within our bodies, and when it occurs, we evolve from an earthly life to a spiritual one.*

Many of the ancients used alchemy, cosmology, astrology and theology to understand the world and to influence nature. This wisdom is passed from generation to generation through our connection to the Earth, the cosmos, and through our own source connection. Many spiritual people spend years travelling the world, visiting ancient sites to unlock the wisdom from the land in these places. We learn to interpret symbols, which act as keys to unlock the doors to higher levels of consciousness. This language of the soul takes us deeper into ourselves and the mysteries of life, through our own source connection. Throughout history, our ancient ancestors encoded hermetic symbols in paintings, tarot cards, stained glass windows and in temples and churches, to protect the trinity and the pathway to mastery. In the ancient mystery schools of Egypt, the teachings were always secret and passed down by priests and priestesses, who encrypted them in the temples in the form of hieroglyphs. The initiates were taught the meanings behind the sacred texts that held the keys to the pathway to ascension.

There is a power to create when a person is connected to their inner technology, and this can be a very dangerous thing if someone is not pure of heart. They were taught to first build their energy with imagination and then through experience, via soul travel, to the inner planes, which would awaken their connection with the divine by activating the spiritual gifts of clairvoyance and clairaudience – our inner eyes and ears – and our natural abilities to heal and to create magic in life. The aim of those on a spiritual path is to reclaim what is rightly theirs on the inner planes. It's about pulling back the veils to the world of truth and magic within so that it can manifest in form, in the world around us. And the way to do this, is to activate all parts of ourselves and bring everything into balance. We operate on mental, physical, emotional, spiritual, and virtual planes. There is an intelligence in our body, in our feelings, in our thoughts, ideas and mental processes. Once awakened we can access templates for healing and connect to celestial layers, to our divinity and universal intelligence.

As an ancient story travelled through the desert of mine,
it brought with it suffering that I remembered through time.
Mother Moon, Father Sun out of harmony,
as darkness descended, I felt it personally.

Blessed by the sacred oil from within,
the embodiment of compassion, from her and him.
When this essence of unity weaved around me,
I started to unbody the Patriarchy.

Heaviness in my right arm that was holding on tight
magically shifted and transmuted to light,
Programmes of wounding that were innate,
created space in my body for the goddess to incarnate.

Heart ablaze at how far I've come,
I bowed down to the wisdom of Moon and Sun.
As I crossed the threshold of a new dawn,
where upon the horizon the Star of Sophia shone.

Now on earth for all to see,
her bright light the flame of unity.

In many ancient rituals, there is an honouring of the elements, earth air, water and fire, and the sun and the moon. The sun connects us to our inner light and feeds us with vitality and life. The moon affects our inner waters and psychic abilities. The energy between the earthly realm and the spirit realm is most prominent at sunrise and sunset. If you've ever sat out at these times, you'll have noticed a profound shift in the atmosphere, which you can feel in the air. It's like a deep stillness that calls you in. The world feels very serene and peaceful. The ancients used the stillness of these times to create and activate magic. This is why many indigenous people hold ceremonies around the falling of the sun and the rising of the moon. It's a time when people can easily quieten their minds and travel within. The sun and the moon always dance together, reminding us to connect to our own playful rhythms within.

To tune into the different energetic qualities inside our bodies and observe how they are reflected in the world around us: to sense and feel the energy of passion and joy, is like watching a glorious sunset. When you touch upon such feelings, you give power and strength to making your dreams come true. Just like the delicate blooming of an early morning sun peeking through the clouds, it may touch upon an exquisite softness inside that connects you to your intuition. You are of nature. You are powered by the elements: by the sun and the moon, and by your own connection to your divine essence that is within your heart.

Chapter 3

The Labyrinth of Love

❖

Myths of the Great Goddess bring life sanctity,
for her breath is the source of all humanity.
When we start to remember we're never alone,
she awakens the ancestors in our bones.

This mystical dance as energy spirals,
flowing through nature and women's monthly cycles.
Bringing blessings from above and below,
gifts of the Triple Goddess to bestow.

Ever present for she is known,
as the Maiden, the Mother and the Crone.
The Maiden, full of curiosity,
enchanted by new beginnings and gaiety.

The Mother, abundant and fertile,
nurturing and full of style.

The Crone, her wisdom never fails,
revealing truths from beyond the veils.

As you awaken to life, you will start to experience the rhythms of nature flowing through you, like a spiralling movement of consciousness, with both high and low points. You learn to walk your own labyrinth that is connected to the organic matrix that flows through the new Earth. You go deeper into the heart, into your own intelligence, to the central sun at the centre of your labyrinth that pulses through the heart of nature. This connection exists at the frequency of pure love, not in what others tell you, but in what your heart tells you. Every day you wake up, you build your own unique world around you based on the strength that comes from the heart of nature within you. This requires personal responsibility and authenticity because only you can perceive and breathe each moment of your life into existence. This means you have to stand strong in what you believe is true for you. You will go through a transition period when the old world falls away, and *everything that you are not* is reflected in the hall of mirrors around you. This is a very testing time. It's like the old you is teasing you, inviting you back into the ghost of who you used to be. However, you are not that person anymore. But as you re-embody Mother Earth Consciousness, you become more enmeshed in nature's principles and the images around you start to fade and change as you get stronger and stronger. This connection to your heart is what brings your mind, body and spirit into one. When the union occurs, the denser world that no longer aligns with nature's principles starts to fall away and you return to your divine blueprint, as nature intended.

As the soul goes through this evolutionary process into higher states of consciousness, you get to meet and explore yourself through memories of the past, moments in the present and dream states in the future. You learn about the nature of reality in the inner realms, through experiential learning, and through imagery, folklore, myth, legends and storytelling. This is where you learn about your strength and power, weakness and vulnerabilities. You categorise and label things, identify and resonate with life experiences and put things in order to try and make sense of the information as it flows through you. You make assumptions, associations and judgements without really realising that your view of the world is primarily driven by programmes that run in the background of your lives. The Truth is we are all conditioned without knowing it. And we are all part of the collective conditioning that is unravelling at this time.

I liken the Goddess pathway to the 3 stages of the soul's evolution that connect you to Mother Earth Consciousness and the 5 elements. There is the Maiden stage, the seeding of new beginnings as you start to shift and change. Then the Mother stage, as you grow, mature and find fulfilment in life. And the Crone stage, the ending and harvesting of wisdom, to be given back to nature. Nature always decides what is right for you as you walk the Labyrinth of Love, and you must accept this as being the right path for you at any given moment . Often, life will take you back into the past to connect to your ancestors and archetypal energies so that healing can occur. The journey into the past may not be easy, but you are taken there to clear the way for your future: to remember the stories and learn from the wisdom behind the words.

Girl of wonder fill my boots,
I feel the Maiden in my Celtic Roots.

Mystical dreamer, hopeless romantic,
if truth be known she's a little bit frantic.
With fiery passion she has manifest
a life for herself that few could contest.
Travelling the world for inspiration,
her heart as home is her destination

Living simply by the beach
the ocean helps her to retreat.
The wind blows through her when it's time to play,
change is inevitable there's no more to say.

Her lesson in life is to not take things seriously,
connect to the Earth, have fun, feel the mystery.

Whenever I journeyed into the past I felt the essence of the Maiden in my beginnings, in my Celtic roots. I was born to natives of Ireland and whenever I travel back in time to my homeland, I sense a deep mystical, almost romantic quality in the air, as the smell of burning peat, a centuries-old tradition, connects me to bygone days. The earthy smell of the peat briquettes reminds me of my grandmother who had the steely nature of a generation of women who had more mouths to feed than purse strings could stretch. Nevertheless, she got on with the job at hand, smoking her Woodbine cigarettes, never moaning. This balance of water and fire that the Maiden epitomises shows in my need for solitude and quiet reflection, which is balanced with my desire to socialise and create. There are times when I absolutely need to be alone and retreat from the world and everything and everyone in it, so I can listen to the quiet voice within. And there are times when I need to be present among others and actively out in the world, sharing myself with friends and loved ones. If I don't get this balance right, I physically feel myself being pulled away from my core and this results in feelings of stress, anger and agitation. When this happens, the universe normally gifts me a way out, by either shutting me down or switching me on. So, if my soul is craving solitude and I don't honour this desire, the chances are I will get sick or something will happen that forces me to retreat and slow down. And if I've been in my own bubble for too long and the pendulum has swung the other way, I can feel myself going a bit stir-crazy, as if I'm gasping for air and my brain is about to explode. When this happens, I usually feel the need to get away from myself, which often involves going out and meeting friends. The Maiden has taught me the gift of balance and how life is only complete when all aspects of the self are honoured and lived fully.

Sorceress of life, eternal gestation,
Gaia gives birth to all of creation.
Mother is with you in all incarnations,
She is the rock of your foundations.

Fertile womb where magic's created,
she comes in words that keep me captivated.
My blood is thick with the story of Lady Sahra,
but who is this biblical woman in the tiara?

She sent me on a quest for the Holy Grail,
revealing secrets from beyond the veil.
The sacred journey that was within,
to become one with the noble masculine.

The Mother is a metaphor for life itself, as it chases you through your various incarnations, from one existence to another. It is the essence of continuity and the presence of intuition; it is when you get those 'Aha!' moments and everything falls into place, and you stop chasing and pushing up against life. She embodies the essence of faith and epitomises the saying, "If it's meant to be, it will be." She presents herself through symbolism as a Golden Dragon, fiery, loyal, unpredictable and fierce. *Her energy is akin to the spirit of the soul, which is there to serve you but can never be tamed.* She will bitch-slap you, if you try to control her, stopping you in your tracks, showing you who's boss. Riding the dragon is not for the faint-hearted, but it is extremely exhilarating. You have to ride your dragon with fierce grace. And every time you come off, which you will, many times, the Great Mother, who is ever present, will teach you to climb back on and start riding again.

Woman of the wild as she gets older,
pillar of strength, the Crone is my shoulder.
Wisdom of the sage in my bones,
help me face challenges and bring me home.

Looking in the mirror at my ageing face
through wrinkles and grey hair, she gives me grace.
As I battle with ego to hold onto my youth,
Turning 50, a time of honest truth.

This conditioning that we have in our society,
values women on looks and it ran through me.
Crone whispers, "Wear your age with pride,
know that your beauty comes from inside."

I see the Crone as the essence of my higher self, very much on the outside looking in, happy to be on the fringes of society. But she is also a great protective force for those on Earth who worship her to keep evil spirits away. The Crone lights the way for other women to follow; she holds the secrets of life, death and rebirth. Through her experience of life, she can take you to the mysteries of the other side. She has often been portrayed as an ugly old witch, bent over a cane with warts on her nose. However, the truth is that this imagery only came into the subconscious mind and then, conscious reality after the Catholic church did its best to wipe her out during the witch hunts. Myths of the Crone teach us about the journey through the shadow world of darkness into the light and about nature's eternal cycles of death and rebirth. The Crone's wisdom tells us that love is stronger than death, and despite your travails, she demonstrates the power that love has in helping us change. As I enter my fifties, I feel the wisdom of the Crone in my bones and in the very air I breathe as I work with the shadow aspects of myself, to heal the wounds of my past.

My hair tells a story that's been hidden in time,
a story that lives in your heart and mine.
The key to illumination that few share,
pure wisdom held through the power of hair.

As we let go of ageism and other taboos,
we invite the soul to embrace a new worldview.
Where the essence of being is felt through the heart,
and in all others who we embrace from the start.

May you find strength to be your authentic self,
and find true love when you know thyself.

The principles of nature hold the secrets to life that cannot be told. It has to be felt through the heart. This inner wisdom that comes when you are connected to your true nature is unique and personal to each individual, and can only be conveyed through experience. Scholars attempt to explain what this life force is, but the truth is it cannot be understood. It has infinite aspects and thousands of names; it is the manifest and unmanifest, the seen and the unseen, it is the world and all the things in it: the stars and planets, the moon and sun, the oceans and land, the plants and trees, the man and woman, and the mind and soul. Once the veil has been pierced, and you connect within, you start to feel her influence in *everything* you do. There is no turning back. When your heart is open you feel a lot more. You connect deeper to the source, and by doing so, you act as a conduit for healing, for yourself and others, because you have transmuted your own pain and suffering, and carry more love inside. The love that you hold can be felt by others and actively switch on their own self-healing capabilities within their hearts. As we evolve as human beings, we move from our reptilian nature and the lower animal instincts of survival into our spiritual hearts, and our divinity. We awaken to more of who we are, which is pure love, and it is this act of love towards yourself that actively changes the world, one person at a time. But before you can rise, you need to move through your pain, and you do this by alchemising the shadow aspects of your being into love. Shadow work is deep, difficult work, that helps release the patterns and conditioning that keep you trapped in illusion. It turns your inner critic into an inner cheerleader, so you can look at yourself in the mirror and really love yourself again, from the inside out. It showed me how my world was completely inverted and how I had placed so much value on my 'outer' appearance when my 'inner' world was where the true gold lies. When I turned fifty, my sense of self-worth really took a battering because I tried to hold onto my youth, doing all the things that women do to stay young. And I had this niggling voice inside that told me I needed to look good to snag a man, and that really pissed me off. I knew that the beauty within me is what mattered, but the truth is, I often fell short of this belief in practice, as my mind played tricks on me. And this mind game spun me around, until I literally said no more and stripped myself bare. I let my hair go grey for three years and exposed my rawness to myself. And of course, it was when I stopped caring so much, when I focused on my inner world and not my outer, that the universe sent a man in, to test my strength. His first words to me were, "I love your grey hair!" This fascination with youth is a deliberate ploy to dehumanise society and is designed to prevent humanity from blooming into its true potential. Yet, as I started to reclaim my power from the conditioning that kept me small, and work through my fears, my connection to Mother Earth nurtured and strengthened me and I actually started to look younger naturally.

The approach to God in East and West,
is radically different one might suggest.

Spirituality in the East is experiential,
received through mediation and ritual.
God is the abstract, unknowable flow,
the more we ride, the more we know.

Wisdom in the West is through catechism,
intellectual property of The Abrahamic System.
God is the bearded father in the sky,
he's the man sat upon high.

The image of witchcraft is sorely misplaced
as a dark, evil art which is a disgrace.
Shadows cast by the Catholic Church,
the shame inside that we all need to search.

To reclaim the craft for modern times:
a gift from our ancestors and not of crimes.

As I journeyed into the past, two powerful memories were awakened within me. I was taken to the time of the Christed Ones and the story of Yeshua and the Magdalene that ran parallel with my own life. And the shadow and horrors of the Burning Times, when the Catholic Church killed tens of thousands, if not millions, of men and women during inquisitions that spanned over 700 years, from the 12th century right the way up to the 19th. As I stepped inside my heart and felt the emotions rise inside me, I knew I had to find forgiveness and understanding for all that had been. And of course, it was not easy to do this work. I had to go deep into the bowels of darkness, to reclaim the light that had been frozen in fear. As my soul awakened to the fear and darkness within, I experienced many dark nights of the soul, as I freed myself from the shackles of these memories. As I and many other women did the same, we started to become less afraid of our power and began reclaiming our gifts on the inner planes of our being.

The wisdom, which was driven underground began to resurface in me, as the cells in my body started to tingle and activate. I started to remember the language of Mother Earth Consciousness, through the symbols that our ancestors left behind in the ground and in the rock. As I travelled across the world, I found many markings wherever I went, which activated my body, bringing more wisdom to light. One time, I visited an archaeological site in the Western Ghats, in Goa, and when I arrived at the site I saw a film crew, which is not uncommon in India, wrapping up their morning shoot. As I walked over to say hello and ask about the nature of the film, the director said, "This is India, it's a love story of course." As I smiled at him, noting the obvious, he introduced me to the two female actresses, dressed identically in traditional saris. Like Twins. Next, he introduced me to the lead male, "And this", he said, "Is the reincarnation of Jesus here in India." As I looked at the young actor, who had long, flowing black hair and a short beard, dressed head to toe in white; there was no denying he had been cast well. Not for the first time in my life, I had to do a double take. There I was minding my own business, wandering in the wilderness in a remote site in Pansoimol, South Goa, and I stumbled across the second coming of Christ in a Bollywood film. Life was showing herself in the most poetic way, sending me divine signals, letting me know I was exactly where I was supposed to be.

As I started to walk around the site and examined the petroglyphs, I found an ancient labyrinth buried in the soil . My feet took me round each of the seven pathways until I ended up in the centre, at the source, where my arms flew open and I stood still for what seemed like an eternity. Tears streamed down my face and my heart burst open, as I released aeons of sadness and pain that I had been holding onto. Life brought me to that prehistoric site so that I could feel the embrace of divine love in my heart and share this story with you. Blessing me with more stories, and evidence if you like, that when you connect to *your own divinity within*, the flame of Christ Consciousness ignites the sacred union within your heart , and this union creates the Holy Spirit which purifies your soul.

Labyrinths are ancient technologies that symbolise the way you walk through the maze of life, and how you make your connection with the source energy. The Labyrinth itself has many pathways, but only one path that leads you to the centre of the maze, to the heart of your being. It asks you to recognise that life rarely follows a straight line. There are many twists, turns and detours in life so the true gift comes from appreciating the moment and where you are on your own unique path. The Labyrinth represents the totality of all that you are: your strengths, weaknesses, joys and sorrows. By acknowledging and integrating every aspect of yourself you can find inner harmony and balance. The Labyrinth calls you to align with the positive path and by doing so, you flow through life with greater ease and contribute towards the greater good of all. As you walk the labyrinth, it asks you to self-reflect and invites you on an inner journey of self-discovery. As you explore your inner landscape, you gain insight and understanding about your own beliefs, values and purpose. The knowledge you require on your inner journey will guide your choices and actions as you return to the outer world. You then complete the journey and return to the world, offering your services for the benefit of others. The Labyrinths that our ancestors left in the land are actually simple replicas of the cosmic highway that create our reality. The Cosmic highway of energy and light is how your consciousness experiences itself at different energetic frequencies as it traverses the Labyrinth stopping off at various light nodes, to explore itself, before it moves on. Everything in the universe is made up of energy and light, including you and me. We interpret energy as data and information inside our bodies. When you reach a certain point on your journey within, you unlock energetic seals which match the seals in the labyrinth, giving you access to new gifts, that activate your body. As a result, the body is renewed, regenerated, and illuminated. As you open these energetic seals your awareness shifts massively and you develop more cosmic integrity. You learn about the cosmic laws of the universe and the light laws of higher dimensions, of which there are many. But the central premise of these light laws at higher dimensions is *that your thoughts can do no harm.*

You were born in the 3rd dimension where people on Earth have thoughts that harm others and themselves. That's why you have wars, control, power, violence and abuse. In the 4th dimension, in the astral realm above the Earth, the light laws are different but our thoughts are still capable of doing harm. The minimal entry into the 5th dimension and beyond, is the understanding of love. And there are different degrees of love. There is conditional love, where you feel love only if something or someone meets your requirements; you love something or someone because they give you something back. Then there is unconditional love, which is free, unbound, has no limits; it just is. This is the kind of love you feel for a new born child or an animal. Unconditional love is the love that can be developed when you step into your heart and connect to yourself in the purest way. When you do this, you start to take responsibility for your consciousness in all moments. This helps you realise that if you are responsible for everything you create then you will not want to create anything that's causes harm. *When you take full and complete responsibility for your energy all harmful thoughts are gone and no harm can be created.* Everyone who is at this level of love is in cosmic integrity and this way of being is understood and lived by all. From here, you continue rising in frequency inside the body unlocking conscious awareness which in turn unlocks more gifts and sensitivities that help you experience the world from a much purer light. Full responsibility for self is required because you realise that everything you say and do affects the energetic field of the whole of humanity. The flow of universal life force runs seamlessly through you as nature unfolds as it is, like the unfolding of the petals of a flower. This principle of nature unfolding is seen in the material world and expressed in mathematics as the Fibonacci Spiral, or golden ratio. This sequence has captivated scientists, artists, mathematicians and designers for centuries as they tried to unlock the secrets of the universe. The mystery of the universe, that our ancestors explored centuries before the telescope, modern mathematics and Google were invented, is the mystery of life that perhaps can never be understood, rather it just has to be lived.

Carved into the laterite stone of South Goa
is a Labyrinth I had been searching for.
Amongst the ancient petroglyphs on a fertility site,
is where the Goddess shines her light.

A sacred place where mothers' milk is left as offering,
in gratitude for life, and through deepest pondering.
As I walked the Labyrinth my heart flew open,
as She whispered words unspoken:

"Look up, beloved child and keep the faith,
speak the truth in what you sayeth."
Upon this site a film crew was wrapping up,
an ancient love story that filled my cup.

Of Jesus and the divine feminine,
the love of his twin, his secret medicine.

Nature always gives you signs that you are on the right path. You might suddenly wake up one day and decide you need to go somewhere, only to discover that something is waiting for you when you arrive, that makes your heart smile. It's like another piece of the great cosmic puzzle waiting to be claimed. These synchronicities, and puzzle pieces all fit together, giving you glimpses of the bigger picture, helping you along the path of life, as your soul evolves into more of who you are. The deeper you journey into the heart of love, the more of these wonderous synchronicities you experience, and we all have our own unique way of connecting to this source of love within. One of my ways is through writing. When I write my books, I am able to connect to this feeling of love that is deep inside of me. When I hold this feeling and go out into the world, into nature, I take this feeling from inside of me out into the world and the most amazing people or experiences show up, to give me more material for my books. There is wisdom all around that can be felt and seen if you connect to this presence within. The world comes alive through the plant and animal kingdoms, through the ocean and the sky, and through your own soul which brings it all forth if you are open and willing to receive. Walking in nature helps you connect to this intelligence, which in turn connects you to your own true nature within. When you are aligned in this way, you come to a space of divine neutrality. It's from this space of divine neutrality that I am able to access the timeless insights that I share through my books.

As I became more adept at writing, and more connected to my heart, I started to notice that the things I was writing about were materialising in the physical world. As you can imagine, this was overwhelming at first. To know spiritual truths as theoretical concepts is one thing, but to experience the power of my words in real life is quite another. I felt like I was being commissioned by my higher self to write about my experiences so that I can preserve the true nature of my story from the highest possible perspective as I am writing it. There have been many times when I questioned why me, but I understand now that this doubt is all part of my journey of awakening. As I worked through the pain of the past and opened my heart to more love, I started to embody the Christ Consciousness, which is the frequency of love. Love is an energy and when you are in a state of love within yourself, you can manifest on Earth for the benefit of all. Your frequency broadcasts into the universe forming geometric patterns in the plasma, which is the light in the unseen world. This light bounces back from the universe into your reality, creating physical form. You create your reality with the universe through your frequency. Love itself is a powerful physical energy that courses through your body, generating more of itself. As you embody more and more energy from the sun, you have to make room inside your body by clearing out memories from the past. The energy from the sun awakens cells in the body and you experience many sensations like ringing in the ears, stiffness in the neck, flutters in the heart, or rashes on the skin. As you embody more and more energetic patterns from the sun, each pattern contains a light code, that you can translate and manifest into form.

Unfortunately, there are some on the planet who try to distort and abuse this energy in a way to deny people their own innate power that is within them. I suspect much may be written about this over the years to come, and I will address this from my perspective later in the book, but my intention is not to get into a debate about right and wrong, rather it is to show you how you can connect to this energy for yourself. You see, you are shifting into an age where you can embody source as oneness *and nothing can stop this process*. This is a very different era and the light frequency you are absorbing is moving you into a new state of being that has not been experienced before on Earth, accept by a select few. Those who try to distort your alignment to love cannot go into higher frequencies unless they too clear their distortions and align to love. They can only stay in the 3rd dimension and play in the Astral planes. They can't go any further into higher dimensions unless their desire to overpower, control, abuse, etc are cleared within them. So people who have those types of behaviours cannot go any further. And that's because there are people all over the world today holding the field of love for you, by doing their inner work, so that you too can easily align with God. Once your mind recognises that the divine is within, your Christ Consciousness starts to awaken gradually inside your body, and the physical body also starts to transform; your internal technology comes online. This awareness activates your inner most essence, which connects you to the universal forces of nature. When you find *The Truth Within*, there is no turning back and your life is transformed for ever. Even when you look outside yourself for answers, your essence will pull you back in to show you that you have everything inside already. *Because nature always calls in her own.* The more acceptance you have of your own divine nature, the more of your divine nature you become.

The Christ Consciousness is a state of being, *not a religion.* It is the energy of God and refers to the energetic frequency of love that Jesus, was tapped into. The term 'Christed' refers to many things including 'The Christ Oil', which is an actual substance inside our bodies. It is a secretion that comes from the brain, and pours down the spinal cord and reaches the sacral plexus, by the sacrum in the lower vertebra. In ancient times, this fluid was known as the Christos. When you transcend suffering your body reaches a higher state of being and becomes Christed by this oil. This is something that happens inside your physical body and is very real, but I will explain more about this is in Part 3. When you become 'Christed,' the mind works in union with the heart for the good of all. The wisdom that comes by being Christed is taught to you on the inner planes through your own visions, feelings, downloads and knowing. This esoteric wisdom is unique to each individual person and comes through the higher heart and higher mind, which can be reached once the body has been activated. I share many of these teachings in my first book, *My Journey to the Other Side*, which explains how to purify the mind-body connection to open the heart. People who connect to The Christ Consciousness access the *nous* – or Universal Mind, and the Universal Heart – sometimes known as the Higher Heart, Etheric Heart, or Christic Heart. When you connect within, to this energy, you find yourself going into much higher states of awareness, transcending time and space. As the energy washes over you, it transforms you and also reveals secrets that help you understand your own reality.

While living in India and writing about my experiences, this powerful sub-story started to appear on the page that belonged to another time and space. It was the story of the Christed Feminine. It brought me back to memories of the time when Yeshua (Jesus) and Miriam (Mary Magdalene) walked this Earth. At the time of writing my books , this energy carried me across India , Scotland, France, and Bali, connecting me to this story. Everywhere I went there were references to Jesus, and Mary Magdalene. At one stage I was even sat in Zoom Calls with people who were on the same path and brought through the twelve apostles! *Their story like all our sacred stories can be perceived in many ways.* Yet I soon realised that my job was not to get tied up in what happened and what didn't happen at this time in history. My job was to go beyond the story, to transmute the misunderstandings of my life into more love. By transforming myself through the goodness inside my heart I began to learn how to walk the way of love, from the instructions that came from within. Connecting to the world around me from the new space of being, learning to fly with faith and acceptance of the magic and the mystery of the journey itself.

Part 2

Taming the Mind

Chapter 4

Clearing the Delusions

❖

Awakened by the goddess within,
walking through shadows of unknown conditioning.
Stories attached to fear and karma,
keeping me from my blissful dharma.

Buried in my inner sanctum
lay gifts of forgiveness and compassion.
I asked Kali Ma, Goddess of radical honesty
to give me strength and walk with me.

Triggering gateways to my inner landscape,
reclaiming aspects of self that escape.
Wounded masculine, sins of the father,
tormentor or lover, which would you rather?

Gifts right there in her offering,
my soul surrendered, ceased suffering.
With a brave heart, I faced the Knight,
slaying the dragon in a noble fight.

My beloved guides from beyond the veil,
gave me a message that will prevail.
My soul echoed, "You will not make the same mistake again,
go forth, be happy and do not let this be in vain."

Bowing down, leaving the shadows behind,
I knew from that moment life would be kind.
May you find peace in this precious alchemy,
as you walk through the darkness to liberty.

All problems in life stem from one core belief, and that is, humanity thinks it is separate from all things and inherently flawed. This collective thought filters into us as individuals leaving us feeling inferior to others and deeming ourselves to be unworthy of love. And it is our collective thoughts that create the societal constructs that keep us small and limited to the delusions of the lower mind. These misunderstandings of the mind run in the background of our lives bleeding into reality, causing havoc in our lives, until we tame the mind, and bring it into divine neutrality. To do this you have to come back to believing:

1. That you are the greatest version of you in all time and space.
2. That it's OK to make mistakes.
3. That your way of living is the right way for you.

4. That you can achieve everything you desire, given infinite
   time.

The lower mind works by suppressing consciousness which creates a fragmented sense of self. It does this by repressing the parts of the self that you don't want to see, forcing these thoughts into the shadow realms where they become stronger if you refuse to face them. When you start to do shadow work and dismantle these aspects of self they come up into the surface of your reality, which can feel quite destabilising initially. You can feel like everything in your world is falling apart and in many ways, it is, because you are letting go of everything that is not you. So an effective way of dealing with this temporary purging of the lower mind is to acknowledge these thoughts exist and then allow yourself to go into self-enquiry as you question what the mind is telling you with logical thought. Logic dissolves the delusion. Learning to bring your conscious higher mind to your unconscious lower mind is one of the most valuable things you can do in these times. Questioning yourself regularly; asking deep questions helps free you from the programmes that run in the background of your life. Spending time in nature also helps. The frequency of the real natural world, like an untouched forest, or wild beach, matches the frequency of the higher mind, so being in nature helps the process too.

We develop beliefs and identities in childhood as an extension of the family experience and take them into adulthood. If the family view is one where the child is encouraged to be seen and not heard, and thus prevented from expressing their feelings openly, or if their so-called good feelings are rewarded while their bad feelings are punished, then the child becomes enmeshed. Enmeshed children have a false sense of self and develop an outer persona that is at odds with their true self. They can experience everyone else's feelings, but not their own. They learn to hold on, shut down and dissociate from their feelings, as they fixate on others. When you do shadow work, you learn to re-parent yourself and heal these childhood wounds by bringing the awareness you have now back in time, inside your body, as you allow these moments to come to the surface with love and compassion for all that you have ever been. Re-parenting frees you from the childhood stories that keep you locked in suffering.

Learning to strengthen your will is key to taming the mind because the delusions of the mind feed on fear and insecurities. You do this by feeling into your body and leaning into your thoughts. It's about moving, shaking, walking, dancing, stretching, doing whatever it takes to experience yourself from the inside out. Yet feeling into your body can be very challenging. People feel uncomfortable with physical emotions because they have not been taught how to deal with energy as it surfaces in the body. Instead, you try to get as far away from these uncomfortable feelings as possible by suppressing them with alcohol, food, sex, or any other trick you have up our sleeve that takes you out of the experience and away from the painful feeling that you fear. However, trying to avoid what is inside you only prolongs your suffering. What you need to do is stop running *from* yourself and your feelings, and start running to yourself. When you find the courage to face yourself you realise there are always gifts waiting for you on the other side of the fear. Feelings of shame, guilt, lust, anger and jealousy that you have buried inside of you and which you may not be aware of, wait to be called to the surface. That niggle in the hip or twitch in the back, is your unconscious self, letting you know, "I'm here, I'm ready, come get me!" Certain people in your lives also have a way of letting you know what is buried deep inside when 'they' trigger 'you'.

Triggers are like emotional gateways into your inner realms. The people who push your buttons and make you feel angry and cross are actually your greatest allies because their actions and behaviours help to activate feelings that are hidden deep within your subconscious mind. Their action *is* the trigger, but *your response* is yours alone. As you evolve and do the work of reclaiming all aspects of your being, you can teach yourself to witness these triggers and question what the unconscious patterns behind them are. You will start to see the aspect of your life that they bring to the forefront, be it anger, jealousy, pride, or envy - or a multitude of other responses. The more aware you become of your triggers, the more you get to know your own inner landscape. When you become more conscious of these triggers at play in your daily life you move from a place of spontaneous reaction to silent witness. So when you start to observe what is coming up from the inner realms you begin to recognise the patterns and deeper emotions that are looking for expression. You often hear people say things like, "Don't get me started on politics," or, "We never discuss religion around the dinner table." This is because these issues touch upon something very primal in most of us which can spark a reaction that is often completely misdirected in relation to what is being said. These reactions are associated with a deep conditioning that affects our lives, of which we are often unaware. When you start to observe these reactions, they often reveal repeat patterns in distinct areas of our lives. When this happens and we catch it in the moment, our Higher Self points a finger at our Shadow Self, which is the part of our psyche that is suppressed and is seeking expression and love. You can then go back to the root of the pattern and face the wounding, trauma and conditioning that needs healing. This is the work of the shadow and, as I've said before, it's not always easy to go into this wounding and darkness. It can be frightening, and you can meet a lot of resistance from yourself, as your mind and body cope with the trauma. However, *it is your resistance that is your barrier to transformation* and change, and the freedom and rewards you gain from releasing the chains that have held you down - often since childhood - can be life changing. To get over this resistance, you need to use the tools you have to help you negotiate your way through.

And you have everything you need inside of you.

1. You have your body, and the ability to feel if something resonates or not by the contraction or expansion of divine intelligence within every cell. You can move the waters of your body and observe where you are holding onto tension and pain: find the wisdom in the niggles and tightness that your body clings on to and let it go.

2. You have your breath, that steadies the ship, and brings you into presence where pure love resides. In the challenging moments when you get scared or anxious, slow the breath down and breathe deeply into your heart, this helps the uncomfortable feeling pass naturally.

3. You have your inner ears, and the ability to listen to the sound of your soul, in the depths of the inner silence. Listen to the quiet voice within who is your higher self, your witness and your best friend, who speaks loudest when nothing is said. She who is honest and kind, fearless and direct and who will, at times, take no shit.

4. You have the world around you as you learn from others, through the collective consciousness that teaches you what it means to be human. When humanity works together and supports each other, you realise you are not alone, and this gives you the courage to step through your fears and come out the other side.

When people come to Earth they take on 'cosmic contracts' so they can do what the Earth and humanity need as a whole to help the planet and each other evolve. These contracts take on different forms depending on the collective consciousness of humanity and the awareness of the individual in any given moment. Each individual has to process certain streams of information to honour these soul agreements and you can choose to learn by suffering, service, or through alchemy, which is the highest form of engagement. You get to choose how you deal with these soul contracts by testing your skills in self-mastery. Say, for example, your soul has chosen to learn about greed. The universe will conjure up opportunities for you to explore the topic of greed, first by giving you the opportunity to alchemise it, energetically. This means you will turn within and use your energy to transmute the feelings of greed that you feel inside, through silent observation of the self, into wisdom and understanding that this feeling is present. The Alchemist is able to observe him/herself in life from a place of divine neutrality without spewing anything out into the world. They may then turn that energy into something positive, which is always a win for the individual, a win for the Earth, and a win for humanity as a whole. For example, I alchemised the pain of my earlier life experiences into something more beautiful through my writing; by helping myself, by helping other people through my books, and by helping society as a whole by sharing my wisdom; so it's win, win, win. If you are unable to alchemise the energies that come into play, the next level of learning is through service. I dealt with my suppressed grief when I taught yoga. By seeing where others were stuck in their bodies, I turned the lens upon myself, and saw the parts of me where I was still stuck. Many people who go into the holistic world do so because they have unresolved issues that they need to heal, and by being of service to others they are indirectly helping themselves, too. This is where the expression 'healer, heal thyself' comes from. A wise 'healer' will always turn the lens on themself and use their job as an opportunity to become a greater version of who they are. If you don't learn your lesson the 'easy' way, the universe will eventually send you an experience through suffering, which tends to jolt most people into action. Suffering comes in many forms; it can be through dis-ease, an accident, financial troubles, a spiritual crisis, relationship problems, or some other stress, that forces you to stop and turn inwards. The opportunity to learn always comes back to you, like deja vu, as you loop around certain issues in your life until you have learnt what you need to learn to move on and evolve.

Your triggers activate uncomfortable feelings that are deep inside of you so *you have to connect with your body to feel what is inside*. And the simplest way to do this is to sit in silence and allow your uncomfortable feelings to rise up and out of you as you observe them and set them free. Shadow work can be done on your own or in groups, in silence, or through sound, journaling, dance, talking, or just as you go about your day-to-day life. Shadow work is about bringing your unconscious patterns into conscious awareness. It is about bringing the unseen aspects of your being into view. *Shining your light on your shadow so that you can alchemise your energy and bring it into a higher vibration.* The shadow is fuel for accelerated growth. You use it to reclaim the parts of yourself that are 'frozen' in time. These are the parts that you were unable to take responsibility for, due to your awareness throughout this life, and others. When you first awaken to yourself and realise you are ultimately responsible for everything that you've created, the idea of facing the shadow self can seem quite daunting. But life never gives you more than you can handle in any given moment so the best way to manage this work is to do what is right in front of you, as it comes up, and live your life the best way you can in that now moment. People often focus on shadow work when they are at a crossroads in life, when their old ways of being no longer serve them, and they feel the pressure inside to change. This pressure builds up to such an extent that you feel forced to seek answers.

When people come together to share their stories, their voices can be heard and the suppression that many have held onto for years can be released. As you bear witness to another person's pain, there's an invitation to turn inwards and find your own hidden pain, which is connected to the collective consciousness of all humanity. So, when you dare to step into your inner realms and break the taboo of your shadow, the work you do for yourself actually helps others too. This journey into your vulnerability and emotions opens up a gateway to the inner realms, yet most people stay locked out of this space by their own fear and resistance; creating imaginary obstacles that stand in the way of reaching their full potential. These obstacles are the result of unconscious patterns that have come from past trauma. They are feelings and thoughts that fill your mind with illusions that tell us we are not worthy, or we don't have enough time, or we have to put others first, or we're not pretty enough, or thin enough, or young enough, and so the list goes on. You have to find a way of moving beyond these obstacles and beyond the fear and resistance you have attached to them, so that you may find the answers you seek. When we journey inwards, we can use intention, will and imagination to move out of our conditioning mind, into our feeling hearts. The alchemy to finding the depths of who you really are comes from having a clear intention, which happens when you enter into this work really knowing what it is you want to achieve. Then, you use your willpower and ask your higher self for strength to face the feelings that will surface. Many people who come to this work, including myself, have forgotten what it's like to truly feel. This is because we have been conditioned to feel a certain way, labelling some feelings as good and others as bad. Many of us are disconnected from our intuition, which I liken to our GPS - our internal God Powered System – and over the years, we have suppressed many of our so-called 'negative' emotions, sending them off to hide in the shadow realm. But if you do not learn to work with these feelings, you will end up projecting them onto others. So, you need to learn how to face the stories that created anger, jealousy, guilt and shame. When you shine the light of love and compassion from within, you thank these emotions for their lessons and send them on their way. When you accept these stories, and see the eternal pulse of love present in *every expression* of life, you no longer suffer, and therefore no longer attract more suffering. You need to face what you've held onto for years and say, "It's OK, I let you go." When you finally own your negative emotions and stories, you release the *power* they have over you and become fully awakened.

Emotions are energy in motion, that run in the background of your life, without you realising they are there. So, emotions can cause havoc in your life in the most unexpected ways. Feelings are energy expressed in the present moment. They are designed to be felt and flow through from one moment to the next, so that you can gauge where you are in life. Feelings are what bring you back to your true self and the more you stand and face your fears, the freer you become. When you learn to feel again, you actually reprogramme the way you live, as you experience the fullness of your life moment-to-moment. Feelings allow you to become fully present, and they awaken you to the subtle energies of the universe. When you feel your reality moment-to-moment, you become more discerning and make better decisions and life choices. You start to trust your guidance and intuition again and you start to manifest the life you truly deserve.

As you journey into the darkness, you will be invited by your own source connection to explore all the times in your life when perhaps you could have done better; times when you shamed or blamed yourself and times when you let yourself or others down. It's when you can stand in the dirt and shine the light of forgiveness on what is holding you back without blaming or shaming yourself or another that you can then transmute the energy into love. One way to do this is to close your eyes and surround yourself in a ball of shimmering golden light. Imagine the light is coming down from the heavens, and is spinning all around you. Now allow your feelings or memories to surface; sit in your bubble and allow. If after a few breaths, you feel some resistance, or fear, imagine the feeling or memory in form, like it's a balloon or bubble or box. Now, in your imagination take hold of that shape and allow it to move out of your body into the golden light. You will feel a physical release inside your chest as the chains around the heart fly open and the shimmering golden light washes over you transmuting the memory into love. If you don't feel this on the first attempt, don't worry, you can always try again. These things take practice and the key to doing this clearing work is to relax your body into the experience. We hold onto so much tension in our bodies without really knowing it's there, so if you can allow your body to completely relax, you will sail through these clearings. Self-forgiveness is key to clearing the shadow, yet when you relax the body, you will actually discover that the forgiveness you seek is *already there*, deep within your heart waiting to be received. This is how you heal the wounds of the soul, through your own source of power, which lies deep within your inner realms.

As I called the maiden to walk with me,
she felt playful, light and airy.
Hiding behind scars of childhood trauma,
longing for love without drama.

Her energy connected to sexuality,
embodying shame inherited by me.
My view of sex was completely bipolar,
from feast to famine, I could not control her.

Eve, in the garden of temptation,
sexual desire a treacherous sensation.
The virgin, the epitome of virtue,
good girls don't fuck, is what I knew.

Biblical stories of Samson and Delilah,
forbidden love held in my vagina.
Suspicious of this dirty temptress,
betrayed by lust, the real sorceress.

More stories out there, they seem to persist,
pointing to the patriarchy, but there is the twist.
This system of separation and duality,
is overcome inside at the point of singularity.

Projected shadow of the Catholic Church,
healing from within is where we must search.
The maiden released my sexual past,
freeing me to enjoy my body at last.

As you dissolve these aspects of self, you learn to become sovereign and self-govern yourself. And as people do this the need to be governed by society diminishes. There is so much chaos in our governments at the moment because the universe is trying to show us what is clearly not working. Humanity is living through a new era where we can literally let go of the lower mind, which kept us from expanding into the greatness of who we are. When you clear your mind, step into your power, and let go of your stuff, it is gone forever. If you apply what you have learned, you can acknowledge your patterns, shift out of them, and break the spell they had on you. You have the ability today to process through the shadow faster than you could ever dream because of the frequency on the planet at this time; it is such a gift. The most important thing to remember as you transit through this time together is not to judge others for their process. The moment you judge someone, you begin the game yourself. Say, for example, you judge someone for lying, if you go into judgement, shaming and blaming them, the energy of lying will almost certainly come back round to you another time. You feed the energy of the lie with your judgement, which then has to go somewhere. It's basic cosmic law – which I will explain more in the next chapter.

The power of the mind can be best explained by the esoteric concept known as an Egregore. An Egregore is a group thought form, that can be created intentionally or unintentionally. If millions of people have the same thought at the same time, imbued with strong emotions, then this creates an autonomous entity, that can eventually become big enough to develop a consciousness of its own. And the entity has the power to influence you. For example, think about how addiction works. When somebody has an addiction, they have contributed thoughts and emotions in order for that addiction to be established. Addiction is an actual entity with an existence and purpose that exists for the reason it was created . So when someone attempts to pull away from their entity, it will torture their mind and body with withdrawal symptoms because you're trying to mess up its existence. It wants to get your attention, and where attention goes energy flows.

It's clear right now on Earth that we have let the worse possible people lead our governments and countries, but why did we do that? Well collectively it's because we believed we were not powerful enough, so we gave our power away to people who are less able than us. The issues we face today with homelessness, poverty, hunger, sickness, suicide, climate change, inflation are because the world is run by governments whose models for welfare do not work. and the distribution of wealth and resources is totally out of sync with a harmonious world. The harsh reality is there are too many people in power who don't want resources and wealth to be shared fairly for their own invested interests. The fact is there is more than enough for people to live very comfortable lives if wealth and resources were delegated and shared properly. If millions of people want to make the world a better place to live for all, their thoughts and emotions gather consciousness creating enough momentum to bring about change for good. You have the power to be part of that change. When you are aware of your thoughts and emotions you can and will physically change your reality.

Shadow work touches on all this darkness within, all the lies, secrets, and conditioning that keeps us small. It shows us where we are separate from each other and where we need to improve for the good of all; helping us burn through all the bullshit beliefs that we have in today's society. As I started to work with my shadow, I noticed many patterns occurring in the world around me. I saw how many women, myself included, took on leadership roles in spiritual work, and this lead to an imbalance in our relationships with friends and partners. You see, when someone is actively focused on expanding their consciousness, it's not uncommon to outgrow relationships, because we no longer resonate with our old way of being. This is all part of the process of natural expansion; people are meant to come and go; the problem is, sometimes we try to hold on which only creates disharmony in our world. And when you're at a major growth point it can feel like you're in a different world to other people which is a little destabilising and awkward to begin with. As your inner voice, strengthens you start to question every part of your life, asking things like: how do I want to live? What brings meaning to me? Who do I want to share my life with? And so on; everything comes up for review. I saw how sexual taboos, stereotypes, beliefs and repression played out in my world with alarming clarity. I also saw how men are having a really hard time, because society vilifies them for expressing their true feelings, and being open-hearted.

Up against the wall, behind the bike shed,
fooling around, losing my head.
Convinced my first love is 'the one,'
reinventing what love means, when he moved on.

Into my twenties, my life unravels,
I filled the void with adventures of travels.
Then back in London, into the daily grind,
too many one night stands I don't care to remind.

Early morning walks of shame,
fuelled by lust that would not be tamed.
Sending this guilt into the darkness,
what pitiful betrayal is this?

Into my thirties saved by the knight,
wedded to my husband, my dream, my delight.
Despite the bliss, loneliness came through,
as he prepared to journey on and his body withdrew.

He died suddenly on a mountain one day,
my love destroyed, I started to pray.
Into my forties, consumed by grief,
I took in many lovers, there was no relief.

Sex was no substitute for the love lacking in me,
spirit searching for soul, my destiny.
Releasing the shackles of conditioning,
the gift of love was my awakening.

Dancing and playing with sexual intimacy,
A woman in love with her divine body.

As I made these journeys into my own darkness, I could see how my relationships with my 'love teachers' had brought me deeper into my own healing. These relationships helped me uncover patterns of co-dependency, neediness, jealousy, control, and lies; characteristics that were still present in my field, that I had not yet resolved. When you go into union with another, and have awakened spiritually your sexual energy which is a vital life force, can be used to transform your life. And if it is not used wisely and put into lustful pursuits, it can literally drain the life out of you creating a lot of destruction in your world. People on the spiritual path often bond over suppressed childhood trauma, not realising that one person carries the codes for victim while the other plays victimiser. If they know how to channel their sexual energy, they can use it to transmute their pain, allowing the fires of desire to burn through the dross that is within them. If they are not aware of their patterns and behaviours, the union will shine a spotlight on these hidden traumas and the relationship will self-implode very quickly, leaving them both reeling and wondering what the hell went wrong.

People have all sorts of coping mechanisms when it comes to avoiding pain. They seek out perfectionism, materialism, addiction, or they turn their attention to others. So, you try to hide your pain by being the best in your field; or you hide it behind drugs, alcohol, food, exercise or sex; or you buy endless stuff; or you focus all your attention on your kids, partner, or anything else outside yourself. Instead of going into the pain and healing it, we tend to respond to life events by creating misconceptions of our 'self'. We tell ourselves we are not good enough or must work harder, or are not lovable. Alternatively, we experience lots of guilt and shame in our lives. We perceive others as being abandoning, angry, critical, uncaring and as long as we hold these perceptions, we will experience these characteristics in our relationships with friends and partners and develop connections that are unbalanced and unhealthy. Some of the barriers we face when we run up against our shadow are:

1. Pride: This is the belief that we are always right and that no one else can offer us comfort or support. We lose the ability to receive this from others and build chains around our heart that will not let others in for fear of rejection.

2. Sin: We become completely blocked to the point that it is almost sinful to confess our own story. We go into a deep denial because we believe it is sinful to have 'bad' thoughts and therefore we don't see things as they really are. And if we can't see things as they are, we can't receive forgiveness for the feelings that sit deep within us.

3. Fear: Sometimes, it hurts too much to even touch upon the wounds which exist within us, and many people are too frightened to go there emotionally. This is why doing this work with others is so beneficial, as we learn to support and guide each other through the fear, to come out the other side.

4. Lies: We tell ourselves lies and paint a different picture to what really is happening in our lives. We become slightly delusional about our stories and rewrite them based on what we are able to believe at any given moment. This is a common coping strategy that most people are comfortable employing, and it's often easy to see the lies in other people's stories yet difficult to see them in our own.

We are of nature, and one of the greatest lessons we can learn from Mother Earth is to take care of ourselves first. You must ensure you give to yourself, that you power up your own body with resources, with love, then you have spare to give to others. In the era we are in now, you have to let go of all beliefs, identities, systems, programmes and behaviours to pass through the 'eye of the needle' to get to the other side. Once you do, you can re-evaluate what works for you and what doesn't, from the foundations up, as you, for you, through you, with your own connection to source established and strengthened each day. As you step out of fear into curiosity, you clean out all the old programmes and beliefs from the old paradigm and expand your consciousness until you are fully self-aware. When you do this you become a beacon for others to live a different way. You live your best life and give from your excess, but not at the expense of your own happiness or authenticity. Everyone has their own beliefs and stories and often unknowingly people live out delusions and fantasies that take on a life of their own. And these beliefs can cause a lot of chaos in the world for themselves and others. The key to living harmoniously with others is to always be open to other points of view, without vehemently defending your own. And challenge yourself constantly with other points of view and references. As truth shows you something it takes a brave heart to be willing to change your opinions and learn in the moment. this way you constantly evolve and grow. And to constantly evolve and grow you have to be willing to let go of what you previously believed in. Never keep yourself small because you don't want to make others feel uncomfortable. This is a problem that many will face as they break free of the limitations of the mind. But your expansion has to be your priority, and if someone doesn't like it, well that's their problem, not yours. Never ever play small just to keep others happy; it will always leave you feeling resentful of others and yourself. As the lower mind starts to fall apart, you cannot un-see some of the things that no longer make sense in your world. When you see all that you are not this gives you an opportunity to clear it from yourself to make way for truth to come in. Truth always dissolves the illusions of the mind.

To be spiritual is to be a good person. It's an internal goodness that only you can feel, it has nothing to do with validation and how others perceive you, it's about how you perceive yourself. The truth is other people around you perceive you through their lens, and through their connection to their consciousness, but *no-one can ever know you like you know yourself.* Your standards, your beliefs, your structures belong to you, you cannot apply them to others. If you do, you will always be let down, especially if you have high standards for yourself. You see, we are all born differently for different reasons and everyone makes the decisions and choices that are right for themselves in life, not right for you. Remembering this helps you stay calm when others are acting out or being opinionated against you. Your most important job is to know yourself, to fully do you, to set your own rules and live by them. You don't need external resources to validate yourself, because you can do that for yourself. Being committed to yourself and following through with simple achievable actions strengthens your will and supports you in breaking free from the delusions of the mind. You can reframe your reality by committing to what you want and working with others to achieve a common goal. There's not a single problem on the planet that cannot be resolved; we've just got to want it to happen collectively. We are all in the infancy of learning this new way of being, so we need to be gentle to ourselves and kind to others as we take one step at a time, and evolve into this new space of love together. Love is the secret to all things. When you work out that love is love is love, you have the secret to a happy and harmonious life. Love is not a person or thing. It can be applied to these things, but if you give your power away to love outside yourself, you step back into delusion. When you are able to define what love is for you and work with that then everything changes.

When you walk on the spiritual path you are in truth looking for a space to belong. You long to fit in, to be understood, but there comes a time on the journey when you realise that no-one can understand you as you understand yourself. No one can have the same perspective as you; no-one can feel you; only you can do so and this realisation makes you *feel very alone*. This intense stage of feeling very alone and isolated is part of the lighted design that everyone goes through when they become self-realised; it is the point before all-one-ness. It's the point when you realise that there will never be anyone outside of yourself who understands you like you know yourself, and you may go into deep grief and sadness, even desperation, but it is at the lowest point in your journey home to yourself when you turn inwards to God-source consciousness and become liberated from the delusional mind. It is at this point that you become self-realised and turn to God within, who knows you before your know yourself, who knows your thoughts, who knows what step you're going to take next, and is always there for you. God within you knows you from a place of absolute truth, it is the source of creation that knows everything. When you reach this point in your journey, you stop looking outside of yourself for validation, and you go within to speak to God. God becomes your best friend that is all-knowing and does not judge you. You stop focusing on what the mind thinks because *the magnetism of God within pulls you inwards towards it,* and this leads you to have more and more faith in yourself.

Chapter 5

Faith vs Science

———————— ❖ ————————

Science explores the nature of reality
through Einstein's theory of relativity,
to the Quantum view of singularity,
and together as one they've found clarity.

If everything is energy
stored as ever-lasting memory,
then this information called Entropy
IS the key to life's mystery.

If life is all that is seen and unseen
then you and I are all that has been.
Everything mirrors our reality,
we make our lives the way they Be.

I tell you now, time is an illusion
embody this, step away from confusion.
Dwell not on the past or dream in the future.
Be here now, in love as thy nature.

Come into the flow of endless possibility
by raising your vibration energetically.
The wisdom of the cosmos is within your heart,
it will be there in the end as it was in the start.

You have the power to heal yourself
through love and knowing you are oneness.
We all have our own expression of this,
it's not in others, it's in your own bliss.

In spiritual truth, there is no right or wrong,
love is the essence in every song.
You are the world, you are the tune,
you, my beloved, are the sun and the moon.

Scientists have been exploring the nature of our reality, and the theory of the universe, for thousands of years. The greatest minds have come up with two prevailing theories to help us make sense of the world we live in today. Einstein's 1915 theory of relativity explains how gravity and space-time work. His theory essentially applies to the motion of heavy objects in the universe, such as planets and stars, and is based on a finite, static universe. Then, of course, there is quantum mechanics, which was first introduced in 1927 by a collective of professors in Brussels. This explains how the microscopic world works, i.e. the atoms, photons and particles that make up everything. Quantum mechanics is based on an infinite universe that is expanding and constantly changing.

In theory, these great scientific minds would say that how we live and function in the world is far from the reality that we believe we are living. There is an intuition, which theoretical physicists are exploring, that says we could be living in what's called a holographic universe, although the term 'holograph' does not do justice to what they can only currently explain through mathematics. In principle, this means we can be in more than one place at one time. This may sound totally illogical and far-fetched, but that's because our minds have been wired to live in a three-dimensional world and not a five-dimensional or multi-dimensional universe. The best we can do for now is to use metaphors and analogies to try and understand this theoretical principle. Nevertheless, as our DNA evolves, which is the continuous progression of humans, our minds will adapt to this new way of thinking and we will all eventually be able to compute these abstract ideas and incorporate them into our being.

So, what is a hologram? How did this theory come to be? And why is it important for us to understand holograms as part of a book about Sacred Union? Well, the last part of this question is probably the easiest for me to answer because to understand the science behind a hologram is to understand the science of oneness, also known as singularity. It is this 'oneness' that sits behind the secrets of unity and the mysteries of life. The unity path is nature's way. So, if we can understand this in principle, through our logical scientific mind, we can bring this thinking into our daily lives, bringing radical change to everything. This is because we will finally see that we are part of the great big connectedness of life, which encompasses everyone and everything we see, feel, hear, say and do. The concept of unity in the spiritual community has in my view been highly misunderstood. Unity is not about agreeing and believing in one right way, it's not about being the same. Rather unity is about accepting our differences in a space where we understand that we are all part of the totality of life. We live in a world where we are unified by our differences, not divided by them. So if you have a science orientated mind, you may well resonate with other people who are interested in understanding maths, geometry, theories and the reason why things happen. However the more abstract thoughts that I have presented in this book may not be so inviting. And that's OK. The pathway to unity teaches us to sit with all that it, understanding that everything has a place and a reason for being. Just because something is not backed by science doesn't make it any less valid, and vica versa. Unity teaches us all to grow together.

Scientists believe that the seed of creation, or, as they call it, singularity, is at the bottom of a black hole. The search for this 'seed' is what many physicists spend their lifetimes dedicated to, including Stephen Hawking in his work on the theory of everything. Quantum physicists call it the general theory of unification, or string theory, which says that all forces and all things that appear to be different have an underlying common origin. This quest to find the answer to our origins is the Holy Grail of science, the ultimate prize for the one who discovers the truth. Scientists have been searching for these answers since the beginning of time, and so has humanity, in its search for answers to the meaning of life through religion and philosophy. What I hope to show you is that the search for the meaning of life rests in the nature of life itself, and in the oneness that created us all and connects us as one infinite being.

A hologram is a 3D photographic projection. Shining light on a 2D film, which stores scrambled information, creates it. To explain further, whereas a photograph captures a moment in time from our 3D reality and records it in a static 2D form, a hologram is a way of encoding 3D information into 2D form and then recreating it at will, so that it looks just like a 3D structure. The information that creates holograms is then stored on the surface of the film. It is this aspect of holograms that scientists are curious about, and why they've arrived at the theory that we could be living in a holographic universe, as holograms behave in the same way as black holes.

So, what do we know about black holes? A black hole is an area of space that is super dense in matter. The gravitational pull is so strong that not even light can escape. Black holes appear all over our universe and suck up more and more mass by pulling in stars and planets, plus anything else that gets close to them. There is an area around a black hole called the event horizon, which is the point of no return. Anything that gets caught in this will remain trapped. This is because to get out of the event horizon, you have to exceed the speed of light, which is impossible. Thus, space itself falls into the black hole.

Professor Stephen Hawking's theory of exploding black holes says that information that goes into a black hole is lost forever but many scientists disagree with this theory because the first law of physics states that energy is never lost. This means that information, which is energy, must last forever. For decades, Hawking's discovery created a great deal of controversy and divide within the scientific community, and it opened the door to endless exploration from scientists from both fields – the classic and quantum – who were determined to prove the other wrong. On the one hand, they both agreed that black holes evaporate and disappear, which would suggest Hawking's theory is correct and that information is lost forever when it goes inside. However, on the other hand, as the basic law of physics says, information cannot be erased, then the quantum world, led by Leonard Susskind, a professor at Stanford University, argues that information must remain. But if so, where does it all go? The quantum world duly sets about finding answers to this question.

Information that is hidden from us is called entropy. It is stored within things that are too small to see. This hidden information is an enigma – something that I will talk about later when I talk about the mystery schools of the ancients. In 1972, Jacob Bekenstein, a world-renowned Israeli theoretical physicist, helped shed some light on the mystery when he discovered that black holes had entropy. This means that they have hidden information within . Bekenstein was able to quantify the amount of hidden information in the black hole. He found that the bits (this is the scientific name for individual units or particles) of information were equal to the area of the horizon. Or, in other words, equal to the surface of the black hole, measured in a unit called the Planck unit. This was an immense discovery, as mass is normally measured as the amount of matter inside an object, not the radius of the surface. It was also completely at odds with classical theory. For example, in Einstein's original 1905 paper, his famous equation E=MC2 was actually written M=E/C2. What this means is that mass is actually a property of energy – a property that all energy exhibits. And what determines the property of mass is how the particles within an object are arranged, and also how they move. This validated Bekenstein's discovery that bits of information collect on the horizon of a black hole, and not in its interior. He also found that the temperature at its surface is ridiculously hot. This presented two possibilities for anything that comes into contact with a black hole. It's either thermalised at the horizon, and the information stored within it radiates back into the universe, or the information falls through the horizon into the black hole. Though, as we know, this information can't be lost so an exact copy is preserved on the horizon and an image is formed if you shine light on it.

The result is that the event horizon of a black hole acts like a reconstruction of the same reality that fell into the black hole. So, the information is stored in minute form on the surface of the black hole and acts like a hologram. As I've already explained, a hologram is a scrambled 2D form, but if you shine light on it you can turn it into a 3D form. So, an event horizon on a black hole is like a scrambled hologram of everything that's in it. This is a very simple explanation of how quantum physicists arrived at the idea that the world is a hologram. However, the theory expands to the entire universe, so buckle up, as it's about to get interesting!

Now, the universe is constantly expanding and being fed by new space – we know that it is at least a thousand times larger in volume than the region we can see. We can only view what scientists refer to as the 'observable' universe within our horizon. Accordingly, there is so much out there that is simply beyond observational science. This, therefore, presents the theory that 'our' cosmic horizon is a scrambled 2D hologram of all that lies beyond it. The real 'us' is, in effect, 'outside looking in'. The real us is our consciousness, outside of time and space, ever expanding and evolving, connected to everyone and everything. We are part of the fabric of creation, inside it, and creating it, at the same time, moment to moment. And our consciousness holds all the information that has ever occurred over all our lifetimes, since the beginning of time. It's pretty damn cool. The mind is a tool to process this information, and depending on where you place your awareness you can reach different Morphic fields of information in your field using your mind by changing your vibration to receive the information and bring it into form through the body. You do this through the heart. I talk more about black holes and what happens to your consciousness when you break through new sectors of reality at the end of chapter 9. But what's poetically beautiful to share with you now is that in the paradox of this life, the answers you search for are hidden in the information inside your heart. Whatever you want to know has always been there, within you, you just needed to expand your consciousness to find it. I call my trilogy of books, *The Truth is Within*, for this very reason. If you have read my books you will know that my personal story and the driving force behind these books is to be love and to find that love within me. This quest took me over the world for 7 years as I walked my way back home, literally and figuratively back to the UK and into the heart of love – as I reconnected with myself again after years of suffering. As I turned inwards, this longing, that brought me to science, quantum mechanics, string theory, the big bang and Genesis all pointed to God. The human and scientific search for the Holy Grail is the singularity within your heart. The God spark that connects everyone to everything is the search for love, and it is inside you me and everybody.

Coming back to the idea that we can exist in more than two places at once, the quantum world has proved, through very complicated mathematical formulae, that it is within the realms of possibility. However, they cannot yet prove it in experiments, which is how science validates its thinking. The theory of singularity exists in all textbooks and is taught to physics students all over the world, but in a language that scientists are only just learning. The great scientific minds of our time are working together to try and find a way of understanding these profound questions beyond the 'obstacle' of mathematics, which is the only method they have at present to show what is going on in the universe. And the reality being painted by scientists is that we actually live many parallel lives in many parallel universes, which is a mind-blowing concept.

The story of parallel lives goes something like this ...

This is the journey of the soul,
it's yours to take, you have control.
Which way will you turn, left or right
into the darkness, or into the light?

Awaken, dear one, and know thyself,
have fun, who knows, you could be an elf!
'I Am' outside, looking in,
life is an illusion, there is no sin.

As co-creators you have a choice
to suffer in silence or use your voice.
Speak out, shine bright, be who you are,
a flickering flame, a superstar.

Every time you come to a crossroads in your life you have a decision to make. These crossroads are called Nexus points. An example of one would be my decision to move to India in 2016. At the time, I had a choice to make. I could stay in the UK and continue my life there or I could move to India and start a new one. This decision involved major thought and consideration, which in turn generated huge amounts of energy, as thoughts are energy. So, if we take that sentiment to its absolute core, then the thought I gave to the alternative option of not moving to India generated some energy, which then had to go somewhere. So, where did the energy that went into the 'alternative' decision to stay in the UK go? Well, scientists have been exploring the idea that it could have created another version of me, and she is currently living out that decision in a parallel life. I told you it was mind-blowing stuff, didn't I! Therefore, somewhere in another dimension on Earth, there is another me living in the UK going about my life as if I had never moved to India. One can only hope that she's having a good time!

So, as you can imagine, after half a century on this mortal coil, there could literally be hundreds of other Dees living out different realities all over the world, not just in this universe, but in others as well. The theory says that we move in and out of different dimensions all the time, without even realising. We only notice that we're moving in and out of them when something grabs our attention. This is because our minds are not designed to know all that is going on, as the information overload would be immense. This could explain why some people, who are often labelled as having severe mental disorders, talk about life on other planets and in other parts of the world. Somehow, their minds are able to receive the information about their 'other' lives, though they have no way of being able to process it. Our brains have not yet evolved to this level of abstract thinking, which is why it's difficult to wrap your head around, but we are in the process of upgrading our brain, which is like a vast quantum computer. Remember, though, just because we can't understand it or see it with our eyes doesn't mean it doesn't exist.

To illustrate this point, only the other day I befriended someone on Facebook with the exact same name as my husband who died 13 years earlier. This other person messaged me and told me he felt there was something very familiar about me, he couldn't explain what it was. I had to do a double take and smile as I thought about what the universe might be showing me - who knows? But other than being super fascinating, what is the point of knowing all this stuff, if your mind is incapable of processing it? Well, firstly, your mind might struggle, but your heart won't. Your heart is a hundred times more powerful than your mind, and you can connect with this source of intelligence through your feelings, breath and intuition. Secondly, it shows you the possibility of what you are capable of, which is so much more than you could ever imagine; it encourages you to dream big. Thirdly, it teaches you to keep your conscious thoughts in check, so when you dream big you dream positive, not just for yourself but for others too. When you become aware that your really unpleasant thoughts are capable of living out their own reality (and let's face it, we've all got plenty of those wandering around out there), then you might think twice about the energy you give to such unkind ideas. Trust me, I wouldn't want to come across some of my darkest moments ever again. Ultimately it's all energy, and the reality you think you are living is a story that you interlace with the power of your mind and with the power of your heart. We create our reality by feeding these two great engines of energy. The good thing is that some of these 'alternative' Dees, who are out there causing havoc in the world, will eventually dissolve back to my highest self, as long as I no longer give the thoughts that created them my energy. This is really important , as it's how we heal the wounds of the past. As you become more single minded in your intent to be the best you can be in the world, you create fewer 'alternatives,' until you are so singular in your thoughts of love that this is what you become. This vision of the world encourages you to really enjoy life as it is, to have fun and to truly learn from your 'mistakes,' giving your energy to being the best. For me, this is the most effective way to use this information.

Your eyes, windows to my soul:
what message have you to make me whole?
Reflecting in them the missing key,
lessons in love just for me.

Beloved teacher, child of God,
I kiss the ground where you once trod.
In you I taste healing medicine,
divine nourishment full of adrenalin.

Joined together as one we fly,
soul and spirit illuminating the sky.
Without attachment freedom to be,
Me as you, you as me.

I think most people understand the concept of a mirror, and that what they see is a two-dimensional reflection of who they really are. This is really what science and philosophy are trying to tell us with these concepts. We live in a world where we are the mirrors of everything around us. What science shows us (and what I talk about in my second book) is that everyone mirrors different qualities and characteristics of what already exists inside us - the good, the bad and the ugly. So, if we see something around us that we don't like, it is actually just a reflection of some part of ourselves that is calling to be changed. This is the bit that we really struggle with ... that *their* behaviour is somehow connected to *our* reality. However, the truth is that their actions are a function of our unconscious reality because they wouldn't come into our experience if we hadn't put them there. When we stop feeding these behaviours they miraculously go away, and so do the people who bring us the lessons. When we no longer have an emotional movement, be it a positive or negative reaction, then the mirror breaks. Have you ever noticed how people seem to move in and out of your life all the time? Some people could be prominent players for years and then suddenly disappear off the face of the earth. Well, this is the holographic universe at work. They come in to shine a light on what you need to change. You learn the lesson you need to learn and they go away, never to be seen again. When you become aware of it around you, it really is potent. I noticed it a lot as I changed and evolved into the woman I am today. As I worked on polishing my own mirror, by releasing my negative karma and old habit patterns, I found that the people I associated with who were linked to these patterns seemed to move further and further away, until eventually they were gone from my world for good. This is the law of physics at play. When we open our eyes to this awareness, we open our hearts to the wisdom within ourselves to change. This is really one of the best ways that we can help ourselves in the now.

Tick tock says the clock, what is the time?
'tis the moment to be thine.
The world is your stage, conduct her well,
the past and future under your spell.

You are a ripple in the universe
creating each moment for better or worse.
Rays of light dancing for eternity,
let your brightness shine with integrity.

May you be the best that you can be
for it's only in the moment where you truly see
a moment of love or suffering,
the choice is yours, what will it be?

How we perceive time is also something that scientists frequently explore. Time itself is a feature of how we vibrate within our field. We experience life on Earth, in a linear time stamped way, as in a past, present and future: 3 dimensions of time. But the truth is everything can only happen at this precise moment! Yep, it's another mind-blowing concept, but hear me out as I show you through my own story how this theory works in reality. So, the question is if we don't exist in time, how do we exist? Well, we exist in what scientists call 'event space,' or as Shakespeare put it, "All the world's a stage," and our lives are played out as different events in space, which is our stage. This notion brings us to Einstein's theory of relativity and Newton's law of gravity.

In 1687, Sir Isaac Newton discovered gravity when he saw an apple fall whilst thinking about the forces of nature. Newton proclaimed that the force pulling apples to the ground, and the force keeping the moon orbiting around the earth, were one and the same. This was revolutionary thinking at the time because Newton's theory of the cosmos and Mother Earth unified heaven and Earth into a single theory called gravity, thus giving us a complete picture of nature. It was as if he was giving gravitas to the famous Biblical quote, "As above, so below" – with above being heaven and below, Earth. Whilst Newton's theory could explain the strength of gravity, he could not tell us what it is. The scientists who followed him were similarly perplexed until Einstein cracked the puzzle in 1915 with his theory of relativity. He had discovered that nothing could move faster than the speed of light. Newton believed gravity happened instantaneously, however, Einstein proved that it took eight minutes for the sun's rays to travel to Earth, so in effect light does not travel instantaneously and it is, therefore, impossible for gravity to be instantaneous. So, Einstein developed a new model for the universe, which unified space and time. His mathematical theory tells us that space-time is a unified, four-dimensional structure, which has been tested in hundreds of experiments ever since. It's as if everything is travelling in waves, and these waves create ripples of gravity that travel at exactly the same speed as light.

Gravity is not a force that pulls things to earth, but it is actually ripples and curves in the fabric of space and time.

Einstein's theory tells us that the past and future exist in the present. The difference we see between them is merely an illusion. This might sound completely insane, but it's seemingly what is going on in the universe, and it brings a whole new meaning to the saying 'live for the moment,' because in truth that's all we really have. This also explains why every spiritual teaching I've ever come across, and trust me, I come across a lot, puts forward that the key to a happy life is to focus on the present moment. So, in day-to-day living, we experience time as a continuous flow of life. What Einstein's theory of relativity tells us is that life only exists as a 'snapshot' of moments or events. And these exist in the universe now. And because they exist right now, we can access all the information that has ever been in the universe, too. So, all the information that has ever existed in the past and all the possibilities of every imaginable future are sitting there in the universe right at this very moment. If we can wrap our minds around this, then the next thing we have to understand is that motion is an important aspect of how we perceive 'now'. For the purpose of this book, I want to talk about motion in terms of how we experience our own reality on Earth. How we perceive the now in our human experience is all down to how we vibrate energetically. This is because humans are bundles of energy tied up in flesh and bone. When we vibrate at the lower levels of our being, we experience life in the now as negative. We become stuck in our story, and this pulls us away from the heart centre, which is where the now thrives in the pure vibration of love. When we pull away from the heart centre, we can become stuck in the events of the past and old stories of blame. This is where our old karmic patterns are locked away. When we pull away from the heart in the other direction, we can live in the land of cosmic dreaming, which is where I love to be, but out there we can then become too focused on the future and get locked into another story, which sends us away from ourselves as if we are running away from our core being. The place where the now resides is in the heart, which holds the key to the wisdom of the cosmos.

All possibilities only ever exist in the now, and this is where we can create our own future reality.

What this means is you have to be present to what is showing up for you one moment to the next. If you desire something, you can use your heart and mind to visualise it: send energy to this idea by asking for it with your heart and then take baby steps to make it happen. You have to take action. Your consciousness will show you what to do. Trust is the most important tool you have. You can make anything you want happen but you have to stop worrying about *when* and trust that it *will*. Not in your limited view of time, but with infinite time. This is the secret to manifestation. The experiences that were rippling their way through my life showed me how the world's leading scientists and philosophers had all concluded the same thing, that the secret to life rests in the oneness that is within us all. The remarkable stories I share in my first two books have shown me, as I hope I have shown you, that it is possible to move between dimensions and worlds; it is possible to reconnect in the now with events from our past. This is because we are just mirrors reflecting on each other all the lessons we need to learn. Ultimately, life is far more complex and amazing than the reality we have known. This brave new world you are creating is beyond your imagination. You just need to keep walking in faith and open your heart to it all.

Faith = Finding Acceptance In The Heart

When it comes to the evolution of the soul, faith and acceptance are key to reaching higher states of awareness. When the heart starts to lead the way, the mind becomes restless and unsettled because it is taken out of its comfort zone into the unknown. You have to be able to sit with yourself in the uncertainty of the unknown, and that's not always easy to do. My intention in this book is to explain the process and the stages you walk so that you have a template to turn to and know you are not alone. Nobody has to walk in blind faith, those days are gone.

***

My son Fionn was born with mild cerebral palsy, which affects his movement, balance and coordination. In practice, this means he has to work twice as hard as an able-bodied person to get half the output from his body. Over the years, I've watched in amazement as he has adapted to his circumstances and you can almost see him switching on another part of his brain to work out how to achieve some seemingly impossible physical challenge. One of the most defining moments in Fionn's development came when we were on a school trip to Ivinghoe Beacon in the British countryside. Fionn was seven at the time and was attending a Rudolf Steiner School. Ivinghoe Beacon is a prominent hill, 750-feet above sea level, and it's a popular spot for walkers and model aircraft enthusiasts, who take advantage of the wind blowing up the hill to launch their flying machines. It was April, and the ground was slightly boggy from constant showers, typical of the great British weather. The children picnicked in the woods before heading off for their walk up the big hill. After lunch, they had a few minutes to play amongst the trees. I'd joined the school party that day to assist Fionn, as I knew the walk would be quite challenging for him physically. Little did I know that it would be challenging for me emotionally, too. As he played with the other children, I noticed he was getting a bit too close to a boggy area that was thick with mud. I sensed one of those moments, where I could foresee what was about to happen, and kept thinking, *Please don't fall in the mud, please don't fall in the mud, please don't fall in the mud,* as I willed him away from the bog. As I braced myself for the impending outcome, it was like I was watching him in slow motion.

He lost his balance, wobbled his arms searching for something to hold onto, and then splat – he fell face down! He was covered head to toe in mud and his shoes were utterly saturated in the wet, gooey, earthy entrails of the wood. I had one of those, *Oh God, why does it always have to be my kid?* moments. You know the ones, where all the rotten stuff only seems to happen to your child!

I ran over to clean him up the best I could, stripped him down to his pants and vest and thought, *What the hell are we going to do now?* I didn't have a change of clothes and his shoes were absolutely saturated and thick with mud; there was no way he could walk in them. As I sat, feeling totally deflated, I was yet again reminded of the limitations of my son's physicality. Just then, Fionn looked at me, as if somehow he could sense my feelings, and said, "I'm still doing the walk, Mummy."

As I registered the sheer will and determination from this little boy, I smiled and silently thought, *Oh God, how am I going to carry him all the way up the bloody hill and back down again?* It was about a three kilometre round trip. Fionn looked at me again, as if somehow he knew this was a challenge he needed to face, and said, "I'm going to walk barefoot. I just need a big stick to help me, and maybe you can cover me up." So, I found a four-foot stick in the woods, which he used as his staff, and wrapped my scarf around his body to make a robe. And, as I gazed down at this child of mine, I realised he didn't look much like a Western kid on a school trip, he actually resembled a little Buddhist monk about to set off on a journey to another world.

The other children and teachers raced off through the fields and followed the rugged path that wound its way up the hill to the summit at the top of the beacon. We agreed to meet them up the top, as our journey to the summit was destined to take much longer than theirs. But Fionn did it in a style like no other. I let him go off ahead of me and watched in awe from behind as he walked in silence, putting one little foot in front of the other. I could see him working out the best path to take as he tried to avoid the sharp stones that might cut his feet, opting for the flatter, smoother ones to step upon. I watched him negotiate the brambles that clung to the path, moving them out of the way with his stick to create a clear path. When the trail was smooth, he quickened his pace, and when the terrain was rough and full of stones, he slowed down and walked mindfully, as he felt every lump and bump beneath his feet. Not once did he stop for a rest, and the only time he checked in with me was at the halfway point, when he asked how much further it was. He kept his head down, and I could see he needed to draw deep from his reserves to find the strength and willpower to keep going. As he set his mind to completing the challenge, I could hear him quietly coaching himself, by saying, "Come on, you can do it." After about 30 minutes, as he neared the summit, he turned around and shouted, "Mummy, is that the top?" When I replied, "Yes, darling, you're nearly there," his face lit up. He dropped his staff and ran the final 100-metres to the top, roaring like a lion, with the wind propelling him to glory. When I finally caught up with him, I found him lying in the middle of the grassy plateau at the top of the summit, gazing up to the skies and making grass angels with his arms and legs. "I did it, I did it, I did it," he screamed at the top of his voice.

For Fionn, the walk was just a walk but for me it was so much more. I saw my son travel into the depths of his very being, to a place beyond fear, where will, courage and faith lie. It was a journey into the heart, which teaches us that all things are possible, if we can step beyond the limitations of the mind. Truly the amazing thing is, when we lead by example and when we are brave enough to do these things for ourselves, we have a profound effect on all those around us. When Fionn reached the summit, every child on that trip came up to him one by one. Beaming with joy, they hugged him and told him: "Well done!" Furthermore, every teacher and parent smiled at him in awe, and a fair few tears were shed as their hearts melted when they saw that little boy achieve his goal of getting to the top of the hill. Later that evening, I received an email from Fionn's class teacher at Steiner, who said she had never been so inspired by the sheer strength of a child's spirit to overcome adversity.

As I sat down one day with my curious child,
he presented a theory as spirit smiled.
"Mummy, what if the mind is the second heart,"
can you imagine the wisdom that it would impart?

This is the gift from our children today
who come to Earth with divine DNA.
Reflecting aspects when grown-ups are mistaken,
small acts in a world that we have forsaken.

Dear children of the golden age,
please shine your orbs, cut through our rage.
Teach us warriors not to fight!
Let us honour the paths that your flames ignite.

Our children really do bring hope to the world. They have amazing hearts and gifted minds, which can see beyond the conditioning that has kept us in chains for years. On the journey home from school one evening, I talked to my son about the concept of a holographic universe, which I was in the process of writing about. He said, "I believe that before I came into this body, I lived on a parallel planet, like a spitting image of the world, no different to the one I live in now. Mummy, you are a copy of the real you, and you came into your body, which revolves around you and I came into this body and a world which revolves around me."

As he blew his cheeks out for a moment and considered what he had just said, he looked at me as if he'd just let me into some momentous secret. Then he tried to explain himself again. "You can't process it into words, Mummy, it's complex because it is in my mind. You're not seeing me, I'm not seeing you. We will never see the entire person. We only see the mirror image of them." I smiled at him, almost laughing at the enormous wisdom inside my son's mind, as I knew I was witnessing a moment of genius. "It's called a holographic universe, Fionn," I replied. "Science is only just discovering it, and it's all part of quantum physics." He looked at me as if to say, "What is it with you adults and labels?" I saw his mind ticking over, as he said, "I don't understand what quantum physics is, but I think I literally just described something under the quantum physics' label. I can't put it into language and I'm only giving you a tiny piece of the theory ... I can visualise it, but I can't explain it through words." And with that, he was done. I could sense that wherever he was drawing his wisdom from, it had literally drained him for a few brief seconds. "Mummy, I'm going to go to my room and regenerate now." He went for a five-minute nap before he headed downstairs to the pool just a normal boy doing his thing.

***

Rudolf Steiner was a spiritual scientist,
bringing forth truth that really does exist.
The etheric heart, an organ of possibility
connecting mankind to all eternity.

Through our blood runs the Christ Consciousness,
activated in initiates who walk in oneness.
Represented symbolically by the bee,
she appears for those with eyes that see.

The elixir of life, this energetic gold
runs through our hearts for all to behold.
Rays of light in our electromagnetic field
transform all of those who yield.

The higher heart is how we access the eternal consciousness of the cosmos. Before we come to Earth and into our physical bodies, we exist in the world of spirit and soul, where the experience is very different and the laws of the physical world do not apply. I talked about this in my second book, *Dying and the Art of Being*, where I described the *Bardo of Becoming* and how the soul can travel instantly from one continent to another, between different time zones and through mountains. Our senses are also nine times more alert in these realms than on Earth. When we come into the physical body, we experience life on earth through our senses and the laws of nature. Nevertheless, before we come into the embryo and rebirth as a new being inside our mother's womb, we take with us our ethereal bodies, which are imprints of the universe itself. This appears in image form as a halo of golden light, complete with stars, the zodiac, the sun and the moon. This cosmic, etheric body remains with us until the seventh year, when we lose our first teeth and this cosmic sphere becomes recognisable for those who have eyes that can see. From the ages of seven to fourteen, the cosmic stars start to dissolve inwards, into rays that collect in the human etheric body around the physical heart. Up until the age of fourteen, we inherit within our cosmic being all the wisdom of the cosmos – this is like having the universal soul within our body. After this age, we develop our own etheric heart, in which the physical heart is suspended. At the same time, we come to Earth with our subtle body, which has within it the blueprint of all the lives that have been before and all the wisdom from our ancestors. The subtle body is a bit like the surface of the black hole, and it absorbs everything we do here on Earth. So, every thought or action is energetically inscribed in the subtle body, which radiates inwards and meets at the centre, in the etheric heart. By the time we reach puberty, a joining of the forces of the cosmos takes place in our etheric body, the forces of the subtle body and all that we create and do on Earth. Within the heart, we have, in effect, a union of Heaven and Earth (all that is above and below) and it is here where the cosmos is joined with our karma. So, when we come to Earth we bring with us the image of the cosmos and we make an imprint through our karma and through our thoughts and actions throughout life. When we die, as I explain in my second book, the chains of our heart are released and our etheric heart floats back into the cosmos, bringing with it all the karma it accumulated in life. Naturally, all that exists in the etheric and subtle bodies are absorbed within the physical body, on a cellular level within our organs, muscles, blood and everything that make up the flesh and bones that carry our spirit and soul on in this world.

The only organism on Earth that actually has a physical, five-chambered heart is the honeybee, and these precious insects have long been associated with the Christ consciousness. The bee is a sacred symbol of wisdom dating back to the Sumerians, who predated the Egyptians. The sacred bee symbol has appeared throughout history, in all the ancient civilisations, to represent the heart, which collects the precious honey of wisdom and preserves it for future generations. It appears on walls on Egyptian tombs to represent the nectar of the Gods. The bee has been continuously, quietly present in the background: ever present and ever knowing. She represents *The Way*: the way to reconnect our hearts to the very core of the etheric forces in nature, to the divine consciousness and the creator, and to the truth within us all.

To connect with this divine consciousness, we need to feed it from a spiritual perspective. Our etheric heart is connected to our physical being through our blood. As we feed our blood and our bodies with mindfulness, acts of kindness to self, loving words, being helpful to others, and further good deeds we feed the etheric heart with love.

Our inner being comes alive through the breath of life. This is passed around the body by our blood, which absorbs this breath through oxygen. Blood is an expression of the individual etheric body. Often in science books, we are told that the heart is some kind of pump, and it is this pumping action that sends blood around the body. This is not so; it's actually the eco organisation within the blood itself that allows it to move freely around the body, and it is this that actually helps the heart to beat. Just as water turns the turbine, so it is that our blood flow helps our heart to beat. Our beautiful, magical hearts are positioned on the physical cross of the human body, at the centre of the chakra system, and at the heart of the Tree of Life. This is no coincidence because it is through our own blood that the Christ Consciousness is received, in etheric rays that stream from the heart.

So, it is through our blood that the secret of the Holy Grail lives on in the stream of etherised blood, which feeds the higher heart and when we start to enter the realms of the fifth dimension, we start to feel and experience life in all its fullness; we become one with the world around us. In some ways, this had been my experience of life over the past few years. The more I opened my heart to the etheric fields of love, the more in sync I became with the world around me; not just with people, but with animals and plants too. As we evolve as humans and learn to feel at a higher degree, we start to feel the collective consciousness of our environment, and all those in it, becoming less isolated from our worldly experiences in the process. We no longer feel the separation from each other and our planet, and we start to do unto others as we would do unto ourselves because we know they are connected.

This intuitive, energetic heart is what we associate with the 'inner voice' or our highest self. Intuition is like energetic gold, and the magic of the higher heart/mind connection was known by many ancient civilisations, being represented throughout time in paintings as the golden halo around enlightened beings and angels. The heart radiates an electromagnetic field that can be felt by others, which is why we always feel so good when we come into contact with high vibrational people. This magnetic field reaches out and touches other people's lives and connects us together as one global community. As more and more people start to live *Within the Heart of Love*, there will be a collective opening of the global heart that will lead to a shift in consciousness on our Earth. Every thought, emotion and intention we have has an effect on our personal magnetic field, but also on the global magnetic field on Earth. This is why it is so important to take responsibility for our actions and to be the best we can be in life because by doing so we are having an active, positive impact on the world.

Chapter 6

Beyond the Story

❖

It was in the Himalayas that more lessons were revealed,
as my soul journeyed on, more layers peeled.
There is always more to discover, this I share with you,
the truth beyond the story, it is this you must pursue.

Pieces of the jigsaw in your heart you hold.
teachings to be gifted as the story unfolds,
"Slow down, be still," my heart whispered to me,
"your destiny is written, have faith, you will see."

Do good, have fun, don't ever give up,
let Gods love fill your cup.
The truth is within you, not in another:
understand this and you will never suffer.

So, relax in faith and complete trust
The universe has your back if your intentions are just.

When I lived in India, my son and I used to move up to the cooler climate of the Himalayas during the early summer months to avoid the worst of the monsoon rains in the south, before returning to Europe to visit family and friends. I loved spending time in the mountains and breathing clean air after the heat and humidity of the south, which got very hot and sticky as temperatures rose. I was lucky to have air conditioning in my apartment, so I managed to sleep well at night, but many of my friends, who lived in the beautiful, old-style Goan houses with tiled roofs open to the elements, had only the whirl of a fan to cool the air and, as temperatures held strong at night, it became increasingly hard to sleep, especially in the month of May. You could sense the weariness of the locals and expats alike, as the unbearable heat took its toll with sleepless nights and muggy days. Most people went about their daily business at a snail's pace, trying to conserve as much energy as possible. The monsoon arrives in mid-June, and with it the rains provide a much welcome drop in temperature, and everyone gets to breathe a sigh of relief though new problems present themselves: negotiating long days of persistent rain and being trapped indoors staring out the window, as the downpours turn the land into an earthy soup. The monsoon brought with it a period of stillness to life in Goa. People slowed down and retreated inwards, the tourists left and the villages of South Goa were restored to the elements and the locals. Everything was covered in blue plastic to stop the damage from the constant rain, which falls like a giant, high-pressure shower and could continue for days on end. It was impossible to get anything dry in the ceaseless humidity and relentless rain. Rainwater seeped into everything and the walls of most houses become soggy. In traditional homes, the water can even come up through the floors, and the dank smell of mould soon starts to infiltrate the buildings, leaving its mark in the form of black stains all over the paintwork of the fading, pretty coloured houses. It was a challenge just to keep clean, dry and sane during the monsoon in Goa, which is why most expats left for the easier climates of the Himalayas in Northern India, or Europe if they're lucky enough to have somewhere to stay over the summer months.

We spent our time in the North in a small village called Dharamkot, just above Dharamshala, which is where the Dalai Lama had his home in exile in India, along with thousands of other Tibetan refugees. The Dalai Lama lives in an area called McLeod Ganj, and I had developed a deep fascination for the Tibetan story and culture ever since I was a little girl. While we lived in India, my son received treatment from a specialist Bone and Body Clinic to help with his cerebral palsy. The clinic also moved to the Himalayas in the summer months, and they became like family to us. They specialise in the holistic treatment of injuries to the spine and joints including conditions such as scoliosis, osteoarthritis, ligament tears and other sports injuries, degenerative disc disorders and even paralysis. Their treatment system is derived from the indigenous healing and martial art traditions of Manipur, India. They use manual manipulation therapies, a unique stretching rehabilitation programme, and natural medicines to bring the whole body back into balance. I stumbled across the clinic, almost by accident, when I first arrived in Goa, and like most gifts in life, it came to me unexpectedly. I had always battled with Fionn's physio regime, as his little legs and body needed stretching daily to prevent the spasticity in his muscles. He is a very strong-willed boy and it's fair to say he was not a fan of exercises at home, and more often than not we would end up fighting as he cried in tears of pain and frustration for me to leave him alone. His daily exercises became a real challenge for both of us. For him, physically, and for me, emotionally, as I begged the pain to go away and questioned why it had to be so bloody difficult. It was like Fionn was carrying the pain of my emotional turmoil in his own little body. When we found the Bone and Body Clinic all that changed! They welcomed us and gave their time and healing magic to my little boy after school every single day. I watched in awe as they stretched and pulled away his scoliosis and worked on dropping his hips so that his feet were firmly planted on the floor. The clinic became one of my sacred spaces in India, and every day I sat in humble gratitude as I watched the maestro and his team work in the open-air dojo in the jungle, amazed at how dedicated they are to be of service to others. The term dojo literally means 'Place of the Way' and somehow I knew that being in the clinic was just as important for my soul as it was for my son's body. With every stretch and yelp, I felt the progress he was making in my heart, as it called me to face my own will and ego. Watching him gave me the strength to carry on in my own work. When at times I was tired or frustrated with my writing, I thought of Fionn's travails in the dojo, and it gave me the proverbial kick I needed to get on with the task at hand. I was mesmerised by his courage when he summoned superhero strength to get his right foot to the floor when it refused to comply, determined not to let it beat him. At times I cried deep sobbing tears inside, secret tears just for me, as I bit my bottom lip and put on a brave face to hold space for him. And I was deeply inspired by the amazing tribe of peaceful warriors, who were all walking their own stories of suffering. These were men and women with broken bones and twisted spines and the hearts of lions and lionesses. As I sit on the sidelines and heard them roar through the pains of the past that were locked in their bodies, I wanted nothing more than to help. I do so now in the only way I know how, by sharing my story and opening my heart. As I watched from afar, those amazing people captured my heart and brought healing medicine to me.

While in the Himalayas I attended three days of lectures, at the main temple in Dharamshala, where His Holiness The Dalai Lama gave teachings on *A Guide to The Bodhisattva's Way of Life*. A Bodhisattva is someone who dedicates their own awakening to help others. In essence, it is the belief that one is not free until all are free, and helping each other. Being in the company of thousands of devotees and monks, who had travelled from all around the region to soak up and listen to the words of their Spiritual Leader, was very humbling indeed. I sat on the ground in the teeming main hall surrounded by a sea of purple robes and shaven heads, as Tibetan monks and nuns listened to the words of His Holiness in pure adoration. The talk was translated into various languages, and I tried to listen in on a rather dated transmitter radio that I'd rented from a gift shop inside the main complex. I spent most of the time fiddling with the dial unable to tune into the English channel. As I looked around me, I saw other tourists twiddling with their radios too, no doubt experiencing similar technical issues. I wondered if this was all part of an elaborate game to still the mind and decided to just chill and soak up the atmosphere instead. The talks lasted three hours each day and in the 20-minute intervals we had a chance to stretch our legs and grab a cup of hot, sweet, milky chai. During the tea-break proceedings everyone got out their homemade picnics and shared food around the hall. The gentleness and hospitality of the Tibetan people shone through as I watched on with curiosity making eye contact for a second with the odd monk here and there. I sensed they were just as curious about me as I was about them. As my mind wandered I imagined there were some interesting stories behind those purple robes and shaven heads. Watching from my vantage point at the back of the main hall I wondered what had brought them to monastic life. To a calling that appealed to me on some level, although I never seriously considered it because of family life and children. But as I scanned the bald heads I couldn't help but notice that despite the veil of conformity from their robes every single person had an individuality that really stood out. I wondered if there were any rebel monks in the ranks who liked to party and get drunk every now and then – I guess there must have been. As I thought about my own life I couldn't help but admire people who can fall into line, so to speak, and give themselves so completely to service. In my opinion that takes real courage. When you become a monk or a nun you strip everything away leaving your identity exposed and raw to be seen and worked on. It is the identity or small self that sits between you and your true nature and it takes real commitment and bravery to meet yourself in this way.

When the tea break came to an end and the talks resumed, I contemplated how I could get up close and personal to the man himself, who was barely visible from where I was positioned at the back of the hall – I could only see him via the large TV screens that were dotted around the temple. I had had a deep longing to meet the Dalai Lama since my childhood, when I first fell in love with the story of Tibet. The thought of sharing a few words of wisdom or receiving one of his famous hugs filled me with great anticipation, as I'm sure it did for the other 2000 or so people who were attending his teachings. At the end of the second day, I saw my chance. I was sat by the entrance to his main residence where he retired for lunch, and spotted the temple staff roping off an area near the gates to his private complex. Realising His Holiness would be passing by, I bolted through the crowds like a crazed woman and snagged myself a position up front, by the roped off area, there was no grace involved, I was simply hell bent on getting pole position. As he and his convoy made their way through the throng of people, who were bowing in reverence, I jumped up and down like an excited child, with absolutely no dignity at all. I'm sure the locals must have thought I was mad or extremely rude! As he stopped every few yards to shake a hand or share a few words with a well-wisher, the little girl inside was silently yelling, "Pick me, pick me." I *felt* myself being transported back to a childlike wonder, as the effect of his presence, and the devotion of the Tibetan people activated a part of me that was dormant inside. The young girl in me, who had given her heart and admiration to this Buddhist figurehead, came back home to self. I felt an immense energy bubble up inside me, it was palpable and vast, like ocean waves washing over me. As spontaneous tears of joy poured down my face and stained the floor around me, I was utterly humbled by the experience.

I have come to learn, many times since, that humility is an essential key to opening the door to our hearts, alongside gratitude. In the process of becoming who we are, before we can reclaim the love that we innocently gave to others, there is often a humbling process where we get to meet ourselves in the fullness of that love. Many Spiritual leaders, Gurus, and people in positions of authority act as conduits for the power that we are not yet ready to hold for our self. When we come into our hearts more deeply, we can reclaim our sovereign right to this power, remembering that there are ever more lessons to learn, doors to open and pieces of ourselves to be reclaimed.

As I reflected on my time in the mountains, I started to see how I had given so much of my power to spiritual systems that just took me further away from my true nature. I was fascinated by the stories and myths in Tibetan, Hindu and early Christian cultures, yet this love that called me home was not found through worshipping a deity or God outside of me. It was incredibly hard, and deeply painful at times to untangle myself from the innocence of my mind and the beliefs that I nurtured and held onto since childhood, but something inside forced me to look into these systems and see them for what they are. I found myself at odds with the hierarchies and antiquated androcentric practices that followers observe, and this touched a raw nerve inside. It took courage and purity of heart to trust my instincts and develop my own unique personal relationship with God. At times I felt like my entire existence was under attack, and my faith in the good within, went to war with my mind, as some of my limiting beliefs challenged me to the core. I could not un-see what I'd seen and unknow what I knew, and the injustices of the world that revealed themselves to me during this time took me on a healing journey all of its own. When the darkness and evils of the world show themselves, you can either run in fear or walk straight into it with love and compassion for all that is, knowing there is always light out the other side. When you alchemise the darkness into light, you become a ripple in the universe creating each moment for better or worse. And when you transmute your own pain you become a beacon of light and hope for others by being the presence of love and compassion on this planet.

Stories undulate their way throughout time
to teach deep lessons, yours and mine.
Hidden behind the stories we tell
is a magical love and its under your spell.

Handed down by the God and Goddess
seven archetypal stories for you to test.
Touching emotions and our inner essence,
so the soul can learn these vital lessons.

Sent with love carrying a special alchemy,
a system for healing you and me.
Activating each chakra with time honoured truth,
overcome conditioning, awaken eternal youth.

You hold onto stories and beliefs from your past because you haven't yet learnt from the experience to move on and grow. The juicy triggering stories that you recall from the subconscious mind carry an energy that is dynamic and real like medicine for the soul. You can learn from your own past and heal the misunderstanding from your ancestors if you go beyond the story and find a higher perspective of truth, which is always love. Your soul evolves when you integrate this love into your bodies and in doing so you can leave the trials and tribulations of the past behind for you and your success lines. As you overcome your battle with duality, with the forces of 'good and evil' that create the struggles within, the soul is forevermore transformed, not just on a personal level, but also on a collective one too. A rebirthing happens as you liberate your mind from the shackles of the past, bringing it into union with the heart.

Stories resonate deeply on a subconscious level, which is why people relate to storytelling so easily and why, when I talk about my own personal tale, I know it will echo with the universal truth that runs through all our lives. And if my story has the power to heal me, then it also has the power to open others up to their own self-healing potential. When you have walked through your own pain to the other side you carry a template for love and compassion inside of you that can be felt by others. And this love opens them up to their own love within. When you re-awaken to self, you connect deeper to the people in your life. You start to notice and feel the similarities and differences in your experiences through the expansion and contraction in the cells in your body. You feel the patterns and go beyond the story into the energy, pausing, connecting back into your body when something bursts into light within. These conscious conversations allow you to feel the unseen within, shining a spotlight on issues that need to be resolved. As you start to observe yourself in life, observing every moment as consciousness itself, many new aspects of your being come into play – it's quite a revelation. The people around you act as powerful mirrors of truth, reflecting aspects of self that are calling to be seen for your growth and development. It can be challenging to sit in the fire of your own being, and feel yourself burn as stories of control, jealousy, greed, and anger are spoken, and your body recognises an aspect of this within you. It takes courage to allow everything to be seen, heard and felt without resistance, but if you do, your own innate self-healing powers will burn these aspects of self away. It also takes courage to act upon your deep inner feelings, when in the past you might have ignored or buried them inside. Leaving relationships, moving to a new house, starting a new job, breaking old patterns, stepping into the unknown, it takes courage, will and intention to let go of the old and usher in the new. And so we use storytelling, through films, conversation and books to give us strength, and help us understand the dramas and struggles that seem to epitomise modern-day living.

There are seven basic archetypal stories with lessons that apply to all:

1) Overcoming the Monster:

This is the story of good versus evil.

The first chakra and our need for survival.

It's where we nurture the inner child,

who through lack of love feels meek and mild.

This is the story of birth and survival and meeting the basic needs of our inner child that relates to the first chakra. It presents through the wound of abandonment, where our soul feels the separation from self, life and nature. As we learn to love and nurture ourselves from the ground up, we start to see life as it really is, without separation, and find the love in all living beings. We learn to reparent ourselves and take our first step to self-mastery.

2) Rags to Riches:

This is the story of unjust oppression.

The second chakra and sexual suppression.

It's where we reclaim sacred sexuality

and start to enjoy more intimacy.

This is the story of safety, intimacy and sacred sexuality that relates to the second chakra. When you purify this energy field you start to understand how you connect to yourself in relation to your sexuality. And also, how you adopt behaviours and values according to your gender typing. Cinderella is a classic example of a rags to riches story, where the main character gains something they lack (money power and love) loses it, then wins it back again in the end. The Cinderella complex comes from deeply ingrained ways of seeing yourself and the world, and from unconscious beliefs that have been there since childhood. This can include things like: recognising what values you grew up with and what values are yours, and what you have inherited from your parents and society.

3) The Quest:

This is the story of the search for treasure.
The third chakra where our will is the measure.
It's where we align all aspects of our being
and awaken to the world of universal seeing.

This story flows through our collective consciousness now more than ever; an example is the tale of King Arthur and the search for the Holy Grail. We may search for treasure outside ourselves, only to discover it has been hidden inside us all along. It is the search for the mystery of life and it relates to our willpower, purpose and strength, and to the third chakra. It is the work of aligning the masculine and feminine aspects of our being, and the key to unlocking the chains of the heart to access the gifts that lie within.

4) Voyage and Return:

This is the story of the hero's message.
The fourth chakra and the journey home where the heart is.
It is where we return to divine connection
and accept the path of illumination as our direction.

The is the story of self-love and shows us that home is where the heart is, in the centre of our universe at the fourth chakra, which is home to all love. This story is akin to the soul's journey home and is woven into the tale of *The Wonderful Wizard of Oz*. The central character, Dorothy, leaves her hometown of Kansas City and goes on a voyage to the magical land of Oz to meet the Wizard whom she thinks is all powerful and knowing and holds the secret to life. Yet the Wizard turns out to be a fraud and Dorothy realises that it was her own fears that kept her locked outside her true power. These fears are represented by the Tin Man, the Scarecrow and the Lion, who all join her along the Yellow Brick Road. The Tin Man, who is disconnected from his feelings, wants a heart; the Scarecrow, who is gullible and always gets the stuffing knocked out of him, wants a brain; and the Lion, who is a coward, wants courage. After she faces challenges along the road and overcomes her fears, Dorothy realises she has the magic inside to create her dreams. She returns home to Kansas, clicks her shoes and says the immortal lines, "There's no place like home."

5) Comedy:

This is the story of man's humility.
The fifth chakra and how we express our fragility.
It is where we find our conscious expression
through speaking our truth after years of repression.

Comedy is about self-expression and creativity, and it comes alive at the throat, which is the fifth chakra. The throat chakra is where you hold onto all the hurt and betrayal from your past. People are either scared to voice their pain and stuff it down or act it out through anger and rage. Laughter is a great antidote to the pressures of life, and when you can laugh at yourself you soften your edges and see the wholeness of life, which often becomes distorted through arrogance and stubbornness. Laughter cuts through the ego and breaks the chains that keep us away from our own humility. It often comes when you've shed the tears, done the tough work of dealing with your soul wounds and activated the lower chakras. You can then reflect on some of the stories you've told yourself and smile at the craziness of your behaviour. Laughter comes when the little niggles are no longer important and the need to hold onto the story and conditioning no longer exists. You hear yourself say things like, "Oh my God, what was I thinking?" But you say it with compassion and love rather than judgement and criticism. Laughter is light and it comes after you've walked through the darkness of your being, when you've gone around in circles and managed to walk through the conflicts only to stumble upon a single event that's given you an 'Aha!' moment, allowing you to finally see yourself and your story for what it really is. Romance is often full of comedy, and stories such as Shakespeare's *A Midsummer Night's Dream* and more contemporary tales like *Bridget Jones's Diary* are full of archetypal comedy plots that hook the reader through the central characters' delightful foibles and endearing ways. In the book, *Bridget Jones's Diary*, the main character bumbles through life, making hilarious blunders and regularly making a fool out of herself as she deals with her self-image, her granny knickers, her Chardonnay-swilling drunken nights out and her romantic relationships. These are a disaster until she eventually learns her lessons and falls for her very own Mr Darcy! The story reminds me of my own life, as I've muddled through my spiritual lessons, almost tripping over myself as I've repeated the same mistakes time and time again. But rather than beat myself up, which is what I used to do, I try not to take myself too seriously and I'm much kinder to myself these days when I make mistakes, which, of course, I still do. I also try to bring this essence of my being into my writing. I'm happy to share my experiences and mistakes because I'm no longer attached to the stories or ashamed and embarrassed by my failures. I actually see myself as a bit like the Bridget Jones of the spiritual world. This human side of spirituality is incredibly important. Our mistakes teach us humility and gratitude, which are two essential ingredients for the soul's evolution. By walking the talk I hope to inspire and encourage others to step into their own light. To trust their own innate nature and accept what flows through them so that they bring their own unique gifts to the world. *To be human and experience everything that goes with that, is divine.* You are the gift. And you learn about this way of being through your own grace and authenticity. People relate to me because they see what I've overcome and watched me grow. They know if I can do it, so can they. The time has come for us to release the stories that hold us down and find new lightness in them. Maybe then we might one day see the funny side of it all.

6) Tragedy:
This is the story of love, loss and tragedy.
The sixth chakra and how life finds clarity.
As we open the third eye and see beyond the illusion,
no longer dead, awakened from confusion.

This brings us to the sixth chakra, and the story of clarity and intuition, as you open the third eye and see beyond the illusion and into the world outside what your physical eyes and ears can see and hear. Ancient Greek and Egyptian mythology is full of stories of love, loss and tragedy. The love story of Isis and Osiris was central to Ancient Egyptian civilisation, as it dealt with the conflict between the dark and light, death and the afterlife, and the sacred trinity of the mother, father and child. The myth teaches us that the pathway to transformation is the middle way. The union of Isis and Osiris, feminine and masculine, creates the divine child, Horus, who led Egypt out of darkness and into the light. Their story signifies strength, the creation of life and the wisdom of renewal and connection.

7) Rebirth:

This is the story of the resurrection.
The seventh chakra and the cycle of completion.
Our connection to the divine king and queen,
we return to the throne where love has always been.

This is the story of complete transformation, as you honour your changes and marvel at who you are once the lessons have been learnt and integrated. It reminds me of *The Lion King,* and the story of Simba and Nala, Spirit and Soul, lion and lioness, twin souls in search of one another to reclaim their rightful places on the throne, as they rescue the pride lands from darkness. The story is deeply symbolic of the journey of the soul and how the feminine principle, as represented by Nala, the little princess cub has tremendous influence over Simba, the masculine, and it is this divine union that restores peace and harmony to the lands. This is the Divine Feminine leading the way for the Noble Masculine to come out of the darkness; this is the story we are living today. It is the story of wholeness and our connection to the Divine King and Queen who are seated at the crown, the seventh chakra.

When you recognise the stories that come to you, and learn the lessons they bring, you move through the chakra system, unlock different aspects of your being and evolve as a soul, as your connection to the Divine deepens. You begin to see the stories playing out in the world around you, in your community, in your friends and on a global scale. You then realise that you are connected by something much greater than you, which is at the heart of one universal story.

Step into the nous, the space betwixt and between,
where magic dwells and the world is not what it seems.
This mystical land where love is spoken,
language of the soul that cannot be broken.
Come into this realm and see the signs,
as nature dances to the divine.
Stay open to the wisdom of the universe,
it is your birth right, it is not a curse.

As the plants and animals talk to me,
bringing medicine and wisdom as I learn to be,
I open my mouth, my words are rhyming,
everything is happening in divine timing.

And so it is that everything reveals itself in divine timing if you follow the signs and stay on the path. It is these signs that are metaphors for life and speaks to us in the language of love. When you truly understand what is being told, you feel this love in your heart. Your heart connects you to the soul of the world, and you learn, through your wins but also through mistakes, both ways teach you well. It's good to become comfortable with the uncomfortable because in truth your mistakes are some of your greatest allies. Lasting transformation and healing take place, only when you have the courage to witness yourself in life with truth and raw honesty.

Courage is one of the essential spiritual qualities because nobody can bypass what is theirs to learn. As much as you might try, you can't pass your lessons on to someone else. Blame gets you nowhere. It doesn't matter who you are, you are the one who has to come home to yourself, no one else can do it for you. And this also applies to some of the tough lessons that your children are faced with too. So often in life, you want to protect your children and loved ones from hardship, and so you intervene and steer them from a path, which is theirs alone. Sometimes you forget that the lessons are there to teach them to step through their fear and into bliss. Nevertheless, in your desire to protect and help your kids and loved ones, you actually take them away from the gifts that lie beyond the lessons they need to learn. Time and time again I've had to stop myself from carrying out the habit of wanting to save others from their pain, as I know I have no right to do this. By doing this I'm not helping them in their development, what I'm actually doing is sabotaging them and stopping them from helping themselves. Obviously, I'm not talking about allowing a child to walk into a burning house or preventing a toddler from obvious danger, but what I am saying is that as a mother, I have learnt to step back and allow my children to feel the discomfort that is theirs to feel. I've watched my daughter grow and deal with the complex issues around her father's suicide. I stepped back and said, "You need to work this stuff out because it will shape your life going forward." When my son struggles with his disability, I have to teach him to stand in his power and love himself regardless of the physical challenges. It's one of the hardest things to do as a parent because you want to protect your kids from the world outside. However, by preventing them from experiencing every spectrum of what it means to be human, you're not doing them any favours.

The law of non-interference is one of the cosmic principles of the universe and a building block for spiritual growth. Interference is when you deliberately, or even unintentionally, control another person's life. When you do this, you set in motion another spiritual law, which is the law of karma, or cause and effect. When you let people be, you can focus on your own life and turn the lens on yourself; only then can you really begin to learn what life is all about. Everyone has a path to walk, and it's up to each one of us to decide what we do and how we live our lives. Learning to put non-interference into practice is a real game changer, especially for someone with empathic tendencies, as they struggle to put their own happiness before others. But when you start to practice non-interference, you realise that it doesn't feel good to be involved in other people's stories and negativity. You realise that it drains you and you don't have to behave in this way in order to validate who you are. When you stop judging and commenting on what others do or don't do, you hold space for yourself and start taking full responsibility for your own part in the story.

Part 3

The Sacred Union

Chapter 7

Acceptance of All

————————————— ❖ —————————————

The path to healing and unity
is found through oneness at the point of singularity.
As you awaken from duality,
the way of love becomes your reality.

When upon this Earth your flame aligns,
you will walk in peace to a new paradigm.
This great work or so it is called
is to align spirit with its twin soul.

Come out of the shadows and into the light,
this, my beloved, is your divine birth right.

The union of spirit and soul is another way to describe the sacred union. Your soul or energy body is like a bubble around you that holds all the information that was not processed from previous lifetimes. Your soul comes into this life with you, inside of time and space. Your spirit is inside the soul, but it is the aspect of you that is infinite in nature and is outside of time and space. When we expand in consciousness, the spirit and soul begin to work together. The spirit is what I call the quiet voice within that shines a spotlight on all the things we cannot see until one day it is so expanded that the spirit and soul become one. As we work on expanding our spirit in form, we start to actualise our gifts and start to return home to our true nature. *There are 3 distinct phases that everyone goes through as we expand our consciousness.* First, we turn outwards, learning from the world and everything in it. Then, we turn inwards learning from our own divinity, as our spirit comes online and works with the soul. Finally, we stabilise this connection, bringing higher states of awareness back into our world, revisiting old stories and cleaning up the misunderstandings of our lives with our new awareness until one day we walk so lightly on Earth that we create no harm or negative impact for ourselves, the Earth or others.

The first stage of awakening happens in duality, within a self-created world where we discover aspects of ourselves in a plethora of ways. Some people choose to learn about themselves through more traditional methods like yoga and meditation, or perhaps seek out a spiritual Guru for help and guidance. Other people choose to work with indigenous plant medicines, or hallucinogenic substances to reach higher states of consciousness and learn in this way. Some walk through their initiations by working with masculine and feminine energies aligning to teachings from ancient times. Whereas others connect to the spirit realms through external guides and use tools, like crystals and tarot cards to expand and grow. Many more focus on their connection to their cosmic origins and Galactic family for support and guidance on their journey back to self. People can work alone, with partners, or in groups. The choice is endless, and there's no right or wrong way on this journey of self-enquiry because it's all designed perfectly by you, for you, for this time we are in.

When you begin this journey into the heart of love, it can feel a bit like you're on a voyage deep into the unknown. The not-knowing is as purposeful as the journey itself because it is through not knowing that you learn to cultivate more trust in yourself and strengthen your connection to the divine. In this first stage of self-realisation, we learn about ourselves through what we want and what we don't want. Not just for ourselves but for others too, as we develop a strong sense of the kind of world we want to live in. It is this desire to create a better world for ourselves and others that propels us forward and connects us to other like-minded people who share the same vision for humanity. When we come together through our shared hopes and desires, the power of the many is what creates the momentum for change that is here now and will continue for the foreseeable future.

As we learn from our dualistic nature, we get to experience life through the opposing forces of what is. Our perceived separation of self serves a purpose in that it helps us learn about the dualistic nature of separation itself so that we can grow through, and transcend, these aspects within so that we can live from a place of divine neutrality. In my case, my soul chose to reveal itself to me through my trilogy of books, which I lovingly call "The Truth is Within." I felt myself coming back online as I wrote my books, and when I went out into the world, I experienced all the things I wrote about in my books, which was quite mind-blowing to discover and a little scary, if I'm honest! My soul chose to teach me about duality through the subject of the masculine and feminine and led me into relationships where I experienced weird and wonderful connections to the past and the ancient teachings of the Christed ones. People spontaneously showed up in my life to help me along the way as I travelled the world, magnetising experiences into my life to help me expand and grow. The hardest part of this journey was dealing with the shadow side of self, which came out in my relationships with the men in my life who I aptly labelled my 'love teachers'. Although seeing our shadow is never easy, it is the shadow itself that acted as my greatest teacher. It forced me to face my inner demons and helped me see into some very dark spaces inside of myself. At times, I felt very alone and confused through this process of upgrading my consciousness, mainly because I didn't really understand what was happening to me, other than this persistent niggle inside – which I now know to be my Spirit. This beautiful feisty spirit within is out of this world and beyond anything I have ever known. This timeless nature of my being which has already broken free of the cycle of fear and is not imprisoned by the limitations of the lower mind, never gave up on me.

Over time, as I started to stabilise into higher states of awareness. I realised that I was writing my story while being the main character and playing the supporting roles. So, if I didn't like my own story, I could literally write a new one, and that's what I started to do. I could see every thought, word and action play out, almost in real time and this helped me become more conscious of everything I was thinking and doing. This first part of my awakening took 7 years to complete and brought me into the story of Christianity as I learnt about masculine and feminine energies within and without. I gained a much deeper appreciation for the scriptures and the profound teachings of Christ from this time. I discovered the richness of Jesus' teachings through my own connection to the Word within me. I learnt a lot about my own strengths and vulnerabilities as I researched the biblical story and found great compassion for the people of that time. I realised that as I expanded my consciousness, it was so easy to misunderstand myself and others. I saw how I blamed and shamed others as a defence mechanism for my own weakness and failings. At times, I felt I was on a wild goose chase; the story spun me around as I travelled the world bumping into other people who were also following their calling to understand themselves through the story of Jesus and Mary Magdalene. I later discovered it was all designed to bring me closer to my own divinity. Our connection to God and the Divine is the last realisation we have before our consciousness is transformed into a much higher state of being. And my journey into the Christian story was in many ways the most challenging of all, because it brought me right back to the beginning, to creation itself.

In its highest truth, duality is merely the experience of more than one, and if there is more than one, and each one of us comes from one source of creation, we must therefore be connected to each other somehow. If we believe this to be so, then the connections we experience with others allow us to step deeper into our own understanding and being, adding depth, beauty and joy to our lives. It typically takes lifetimes for these connections to self to grow and deepen, but we are living through times of great acceleration in consciousness, and it is this acceleration that supports our growth and calls us deeper into the heart of love.

As we journey inwards, we reach a pivotal point in the growth of our consciousness where we awaken for a second time to *the totality of all that is*. A massive shift occurs when this happens, and instead of experiencing life from our own individual bubble, our consciousness is spontaneously opened to the totality of all. We become aware that everything and everyone is connected to God/ Source/ Creator and this self-realisation changes how we perceive reality forever. In a moment of singularity, our consciousness returns to creation and becomes everything, everywhere all at once. The experience of duality in that moment is gone, and you realise *that you are all that you are*. This 'bubble bursting' experience can be shocking yet liberating, humbling yet terrifying, and can lead to a bit of an existential dilemma. When your consciousness returns to itself, transformed and illuminated, a dissolution occurs on the inner planes of your reality. There is a sort of death of the old self and a rebirthing of the new. It is through this experience that we get to meet ourselves again, but with an even higher awareness than before, with more love, compassion and wonder for life itself, and everyone and everything in it. The illusion of separation is no longer felt and you begin the purification process as you come to know yourself a little better. You can feel like you're going slightly mad as you start to embody more and more of your own consciousness because this newfound awareness brings with it many earth-shattering moments of realisation where you start to take full responsibility for yourself, your story and your actions. You no longer look to others for answers or look to blame others for how you are feeling inside; this early stage can be quite an adjustment as your consciousness trickles into your body, teaching you to accept the world as it is, without the desire to change anything, even the most challenging aspects of life. You are shown that the horrific actions that you previously judged or vilified in others, you are capable of doing, maybe not in this lifetime, but in another. You can see how it is possible because of your newfound connection to *all that is*. Once you've burst out of your self-imposed cage, your consciousness enters a state of oneness and a union occurs between your heart and mind. The mind starts to quieten its usual chatter, the judgments, opinions and reasoning eventually go away and the heart becomes more felt, it speaks louder if you like. The heart and mind no longer work against each other but start to work together with the heart eventually leading the way. As this happens, the whole of your being starts to purify naturally and you begin to operate from an upgraded version of yourself, which gradually brings you back to your True Nature. As we come back online, we start to face many uncomfortable truths as we awaken the sleeping shadows within us that ask us to accept all that is. This can be a particularly challenging time for humanity, but *it's only when we are willing to accept all that is, that we can ever know God.* The final part of this book explores this part of the awakening process as I share my own experience and give you some tools to support your journey into the Heart of Love

***

It takes just one perfect moment of silence to step into the heart of love.

Give yourself this moment now.

Place your hand on your heart.

Take three gentle breaths in and out of the nose and feel the expansion in your chest as your beautiful heart opens.

Now, introduce yourself to your body, say your name silently or out loud, say, "Hello, I am ....." and feel your heart flutter with excitement as you receive yourself in this sacred heart space.

Now, feel your lifeforce spring into life, inside your body.

What you are feeling is your own source connection, which comes from deep within the core of your being.

When you do this, the divine intelligence within your body springs to life and activates the body's self-healing capabilities.

You start to purify naturally, simply, maybe even effortlessly, as you journey back to your true nature.

You are now connected to your own power which in turn is connected to Mother-Earth consciousness and the 5 elements, through your energy lines.

Your inner world – the microcosm, is connected to your outer world, the macrocosm.

It does not matter where you are or what you are doing, you can connect to this presence at any time.

The key is to relax, allow the heart to open, and accept this gift of love.

A few simple conscious breaths are all it takes to lead you into your inner world, and from here, new life is birthed in the blink of an eye, captured as snapshots, each moment building on the next. Every time you connect to your heart, your inner teacher will guide you on a path to self-mastery through your own personal instructions. You just need to give yourself this time each day. The word 'heart' has the word 'ear' in the middle and has the same letters as the word 'Earth'. When we connect to the Earth and listen to our hearts, we hear what we need to expand and grow in any given moment. These heart-based instructions come as inner feelings, inner sight, inner sound and inner knowing. The heart has its own internal compass and the only way to read and master our internal instructions is to connect to ourselves more deeply each day. Our lives are divinely designed through the way of the heart, we just have to keep returning to this stillness within and trusting the wisdom to show us the way.

The way of the heart is simple, but not always easy.

The heart asks us to face all that we are, the seen and the unseen, the bits we like and the bits that we don't like, and it's here in the darker gnarly parts of ourselves where we often get stuck and blindsided. An open heart will show us the ugly side of who we are, through the behaviours that we so readily call out in others, such as anger, jealousy, pride, lust, greed etc. These traits that we are less willing to 'own' for ourselves but so easily see in others are presented to us in life to help us move through them. We move through these behaviours by keeping the heart open. When we accept what is, we move through life with grace and ease as we meet all with curiosity, self-love, and self-acceptance.

The shadow is the side of us that we haven't yet been able to fully integrate and love. It's the part of us that gossips about others when we know we shouldn't' the part that gets angry at the kids because we're stressed or jealous at our partner when they're admiring someone else; it can be hateful and abusive if someone wrongs us and it can even kill if someone is threatening our life or someone else's. There is so much to the shadow side of life that we don't want to see and one of the hardest stages in the spiritual journey is accepting the totality of God's creation and understanding that the shadow is part of the experience of life. And if we deny part of the experience, we are denying ourselves and God because we are part of the whole and it is part of us. When we are not ready to own the whole of our shadow side, we judge others and are less willing to forgive them. We vilify people who do wrong in the world and even condemn them to suffering in the name of righteousness.

It's one of the hardest things to accept in this journey of life, but the famous quote from Gandhi, "An eye for an eye makes the whole world blind," actually explains the concept very well. If we vilify the wrongs of the world then we are still in a place of duality, feeding this wrongdoing with our own disdain, energising it rather than bringing it into divine neutrality, which allows it to go away naturally. As we rise in consciousness, we reach a stage where we meet our shadow so completely, that something inside switches on and we finally accept it as being our own creation. I call this the moment of singularity, or my black hole moment, which I will explain further in the next chapter.

When we connect to our own divinity, we access the internal technology needed to achieve higher states of consciousness. But what does it mean to evolve spiritually, to be expanded, to be in union with the divine which is our true nature? Well, like all things in life, it will mean different things to different people, depending on their beliefs, culture and practice. For me, my soul evolution is connected to the need to transcend 'suffering' in this life. My suffering was very much associated with my birth name, Dolores, and my Catholic roots. Dolores is the plural of the Spanish word, 'dolor' meaning sorrow or pain. The name is strongly connected to the Catholic Church, and one of the many titles given to Mother Mary is Our Lady of Sorrows. In my innocence as a young child, I used to hate my name, because I thought it meant that I created pain and suffering for others. I used to flinch when anyone called me Dolores and even to this day most people know me as Dee, rather than by my full name. It took me years to understand the profound effect my name had on the way I perceived myself in the world. In my naivety, I thought I had to take away other people's sorrows, which meant I developed an overly empathetic side, always putting others' happiness over my own. So, in this first part of my life, my sole purpose was to learn how to love myself completely and reclaim the love I gave to everyone and everything outside myself. That meant I had to learn to stand up for myself and say no to others with integrity and love, understanding that saying no with the frequency of love, is just as valid as saying yes in the name of love. I found out the hard way that doing things that I didn't want to do through obligation resulted in self-sacrifice, resentment,, and suffering. Breaking the programmes of self-sacrifice and self-abandonment was one of my hardest challenges and I was shocked to see how easily I could give myself up to please others. I also learnt that love and pain are two sides of the same coin and both played a part in getting me to where I am today.

Once I was able to accept all of myself, including all the parts of me that I tried to deny, I could begin the process of reclaiming all aspects of myself that have suffered in this life, and others, to transmute these aspects into love. This is an ongoing process, one that awakens the sleeping shadow inside and takes you into the past and the future, not that either of these realms truly exist, but more on that later. When you transcend suffering, you align more naturally to divine will, and the need to control life disappears as you allow the purest path of your destiny to unfold. You still encounter experiences that make you sad or angry, you feel everything more strongly in fact, but the difference is that you do not suffer from sadness or anger because you've learnt to accept life from a higher perspective. When you choose to see most situations from a place of love, the more challenging experiences in life tend to float through you. They don't fester inside your mind, they come, you deal with them with love and curiosity for all that is, and they go.

Love is a *state of being*. As your soul evolves, you go deeper into this state. When you connect to yourself as love, you find pieces of yourself in the world around you and bring them back to your heart. This is how you return to your true nature, which I define as being love. I, like everyone else on Earth, am a work in progress, working on my *being-ness*, putting one foot in front of the other and following my own personal guidance that comes from within. My journey has been beautiful and messy. I have struggled with my stubborn mind and fought my own shadow on many occasions, but through it all, I have this staggering faith that never allows me to give up. It is faith that keeps the light of humanity shining. I describe Faith as - *Finding Acceptance in The Heart.* It's about being able to accept what is, even if you might not like it, or agree with it. It's about having the wisdom to know that whatever is happening in this moment, it is happening for a reason. And if you are struggling with it, it's because you are not aware in that moment. Faith keeps you moving forward, in the not knowing, in the understanding that all will be revealed in divine timing. Pure consciousness is created from a space of love, so the struggles we have in life are created by us when the heart and mind are in a tug of war for power. This power struggle is felt through the stories we tell ourselves, the resistance we feel in our body and the pressures from the external world. It is all created from within. To break out of this power struggle, we must free ourselves from our own self-imposed limitations that keep our hearts locked in chains and imprison us from accessing our true nature. When we surrender to faith, the heart stays open and an open heart will naturally purify the mind.

If we want to keep our hearts open, we have to stay in our own lane and be truly authentic when honouring what we believe is right for us on our path. Put simply, when we follow our own rules and do the things we love, we generate more love for ourselves, and this creates a ripple effect in the world. Our commitment to ourselves is the single most important thing we can do for the world during times of great change because our uniqueness is golden. Only you can bring you into the world and offer up what you have to offer. You have a piece of the creation puzzle sitting in your heart, and your piece is pure gold, just like everyone else's. But it's up to you to water your heart seeds, to allow them to grow and nurture them to their full potential. And it's up to you to remain unique and stay true to your heart, even when this goes against what is happening in the world around you.

There will be many times in life when you have to say no, not just to strangers but to people you love and admire. It's hard when our friends and family constantly question our decisions. When we're not on the same page, perhaps we've changed, and this change triggers something inside of them. We should never hold ourselves back or stop our growth just because it makes others feel uncomfortable, that only leads to suffering and works against us. But many people, including myself at times, do hold back, because of our love for others and because we're scared of leaving people behind or creating too wide a gap between ourselves and our loved ones to the point where we can't relate to them. And those who tend to awaken first are naturally empathetic to other people's needs and might struggle to say no, or feel particularly uncomfortable when faced with challenging situations that require them to stand their ground. But I, like many others, have had to learn the hard way that saying no doesn't have to be difficult if it is said with love. When we say no in love for ourselves, for the other person and with understanding of the bigger picture at play it actually feels liberating and freeing. We feel no resistance inside when love is at play. Sometimes the fear of saying no is actually much worse than saying no itself and often we can be surprised at the other person's response when we say no in a kind yet firm and loving way. They often go, "Yeah, OK" and move on, because the person who is holding on and forcing the issue is usually the one who needs to say no. So, the more we learn to stand in our truth and be authentic, the more truth we become, and the easier life becomes. Eventually, our connection to the self grows so strong that people no longer question what we say or do, rather they just allow us to be. As more people stand in their power in this way, life becomes infinitely easier because we learn to accept each other's differences without being threatened or challenged by them. Just think for a moment how dull life would be if we were all the same if we all looked the same, or acted in the same way, like robots. There would be no joy in learning from another person and exploring our differences.

It's this ability to see another perspective without resistance, even if you do not agree with it, that opens you up to the fullness of life. If you can accept that all things in creation exist in this dualistic reality for a reason, then your acceptance moves you through that which you do not want into that which you do.

We learn about the nature of reality initially through the mind-body connection, and then we learn about life at a soul level. As I mentioned earlier in the initial awakening stage, most people learn about spirituality through the wisdom of others. We may read self-help books, go on retreats, practise yoga and meditation, do breathwork, go to church, or participate in a myriad of other modalities that bring us into a new state of awareness. Turning to others for support and guidance in this initial stage is perfectly normal on your journey to enlightenment. As we start to make fresh discoveries about life, the universe and beyond, we begin to re-evaluate our lives with renewed understanding and make changes where change is needed. We experience these changes on an emotional, mental, spiritual and physical level. We develop more body awareness and mindfulness. Our diet may change, our body may also start to change, and people may move in or out of our lives; we may change jobs, move countries, start a new relationship or end one that no longer serves us. This phase of awakening is like a dance that takes many twists and turns and is not always comfortable, yet change never is. We are changing on the inside in the unseen inner worlds which actually make up more than 97% of our reality and as we start to notice this, the world around us changes, too.

As the body-mind starts to come together, you begin to change on a deeper soul level. And when you embody more of your soul, which is the field around you, you connect to an inner knowing that triggers a shift in consciousness. As you continue to journey inwards, you begin to trust and rely on your own heart for guidance, rather than turning to outside sources and other people to lead the way for you. This trust in self takes time of course, and the speed at which you gain confidence in your own guidance is determined by how committed you are to show up for yourself each day. It takes daily commitment and discipline to show up for you as you. It's not something you can avoid or skip. You have to make that connection to self each and every day, but as I explained earlier it only takes a few moments to connect , so this is very achievable for even the busiest of people.

When we look outside, we dream, when we look inside, we awaken.

When we first awaken to ourselves, we often become mesmerised by the synchronicities that appear in our world, which seemingly encourage and entice us on the path forward. Frequently, we give deeper meaning and analyse these messages from the universe not realising that this too is the mind at play. You see, every time we turn our awareness to something outside ourselves, we are in fact turning away from our inner world, and these outer distractions are really just a reminder to keep our attention inside. Once we realise that the mind will *always* ask endless questions, because that's what it is designed to do, we can catch ourselves when the mind wanders, which it does constantly in the early stages of awakening, and return to the stillness within, as we learn to master the chattering mind. We do this by observing ourselves in our lives, one breath at a time, consciously returning to stillness every time we catch ourselves wandering. Training the mind in everyday life is a practice that grows and expands as we do. You know when you have reached a point of stillness inside when there is no reaction, or judgement to the experiences outside of yourself. You feel in harmony with whatever is showing up for you in that moment. Peace is felt as being neutral, and it's in this state of neutrality that you start to embody your soul.

Your consciousness is always waiting for you in the moment.

When you still the mind, you can directly connect to consciousness through the heart. We do this one moment at a time. Being in the moment is a state of being, and in truth, it has nothing to do with religion or new age spirituality, it's a way to connect to yourself in the purest way like a child does. Many people are returning to this natural way of being now on Earth at this time and our consciousness has a template for us to return home to this natural state of being. Our consciousness is always trying to guide us to this higher state of being. It is not interested in beliefs, questions, personalities or identities. - *This is All in the Mind.* Our consciousness sits behind all of that in the back seat of life to begin with, but as we grow and evolve, as the chattering mind starts to become more still and more tamed, our consciousness gets louder and louder until it pierces the veil of reality, bursting us out of our small individual bubbles into the driving seat of pure limitless potential.

Life is always trying to show you another way.

Once we have established a connection with our consciousness and allowed it to guide our experience, we move out of the needing to know phase of our awakening into the *'not knowing'* phase. This can be a curious and challenging time because it's when we get to clear out all our limiting beliefs and come out the other side. This can be painful at times, especially if we have held onto deep-seated beliefs for aeons. The mind can take you down many rabbit holes searching for endless answers, as we battle with ourselves. When you think you know something, an experience will eventually come along that teaches you something, but you don't know what. This is the mystery, the gift, that makes the human experience so rich. However, it is this 'not knowing' that we so often fight against because it takes us out of the lower mind and our comfort zone, into a new space of being where we can experience ourselves with fresh eyes and a new level of heightened awareness. It is this not knowing that makes life so exciting and rich, but it is also the not knowing that we seem to fear the most because of our years of conditioning so we try to hold onto the familiar, fearing to move beyond it.

Questions come from the programmes running in the background of the mind.

When we are faced with uncertainty in life, we often turn to others for advice, asking our friends and family, or respected individuals who are masters in their field what to do, or we may search for answers in books or videos online. And there's nothing wrong with this, as I said before. That's what this book is doing, creating a space for self-enquiry and discovery, but it's really important that you sit with yourself first and ask why you are asking the question and turn inwards to empower yourself to find the answer. There is always a reason why you ask questions. Often there is an underlying fear at play or a need for certainty, or just plain curiosity from the lower mind that is being updated. The need for certainty is actually a need to feel safe, which goes all the way back to our childhood and the influences we adopted at this time. However, if you have questions rumbling around inside your head, try to pause and allow yourself the space and time *to find your own answers*. What happens is that when you pause and bring something inwards, you create a space for your consciousness to observe how your mind responds. Your consciousness can then be heard and felt, and this empowers you to take responsibility for your own life because the best solution for you always comes from this higher perspective within. Your consciousness will always give you the next step to take. You might not like it, you might not want to do it, you might not understand it, but it is the right one for you at that moment. And sometimes, when you open yourself up in this way there may be nothing at all, no answer. And that's OK too, because at that moment there is nothing for you to gain from your question, after all your question is coming from the mind, and your consciousness, which is beyond the mind, is bringing you deeper into a space of openness. So, it might be that the question you are presenting from the mind is not relevant to the path that your consciousness is trying to take you down. We learn by living and experiencing ourselves one moment at a time. The way to master this is by practising stillness and strengthening the ground of reality from within.

Your consciousness is a gateway to the infinite possibilities of reality.

Once we accept that we can never ever truly 'know' anything, because the infinite is boundless, we stop searching for answers and just be. We stop searching outside ourselves and surrender to life becoming more stable in the not knowing. You do this by being in the present moment, from one moment to the next, walking the path that your consciousness has designed for you, one step at a time. We are all learning this new way of being and moving, in and out of conscious awareness and higher states of living all the time, and it's all perfect. When you first awaken to your soul path, you find yourself side-tracked all the time. You get pulled into the mind and into stories of the past, or old familiar patterns of behaviours that are still present in the background of your life and want to be expressed. This happens over and over again and is perfectly normal because you're training to be more conscious in life, and this takes time, it doesn't happen overnight. But when you catch yourself being distracted and getting caught up in the story, you know it's happening and you just go back to the breath, still your mind and bring your awareness inwards again, connect to your consciousness in the here and now, and press reset. One way to do this is to be very direct, and ask your consciousness, "What do you wish me to learn now?" Talk to yourself as really getting to know yourself is the highest form of self-love there is. Your consciousness will then reveal itself to you one moment at a time. And from here on you take another step forward and expand into more of who you are.

Nothing in life is ever wasted, there are no mistakes as such, as we expand and become more of who are, t we can take the long way home or travel the path of least resistance which is through the heart. In fact, as long as we are being authentic and living our lives as best we can, we expand naturally by doing what's right in front of us, even if it seems wrong. We learn just as much, maybe even more about ourselves when we make mistakes and get things horribly wrong. When we are conscious of our mistakes and willing to be honest with ourselves, we tend to find peace in our mistakes rather than judging and being hard on ourselves.

I see you, visions in my inner eye,
this is the nous, where the treasure lies.
Blessed are those with creative imagination,
dreams are the sparks of all creation.

Open your ears to her inner voice,
hear this sweet sound, go forth, rejoice!
Intuition, chicken soup for the soul,
kissed by grace, make me whole.

There is no sin, you've been sold a lie,
God's plan for redemption was not to die.
There is divine mercy in every expression of life,
live in peace, be free from strife.

The nous is the word that was used in ancient times to describe this state of being, from which the higher state of awareness comes. Another way to describe it is the space of nothingness where everything resides, or where the manifest merges with the un-manifest. We reach this state by bringing ourselves into harmony with nature's principles and aligning the dualistic forces of masculine energy and action with the feminine energy of trust, flow and receptivity. Mastery of the nous is what the initiates of the ancient mystery schools learnt. Today, people call this space the void or the zero-point zone.

We know when we've dropped into this space because we feel an expansiveness inside, and it's this feeling of expansiveness that leads to self-mastery of the Self. This connection takes us deeper into ourselves, and when we bring this out into the world, we start to change the way we perceive life. We start to realise that our true power lies in the space inside us, not from anything outside, and this feeling encourages us to keep returning to ourselves, as we build more and more momentum and spend more time in this space of stillness within. As we consciously create our world from the inside out, the decisions and actions we make in the world change. We value ourselves and the things we do based on how we feel inside. We tend to worry less about how others perceive us, and this affects every aspect of life, from how you spend your time to how you treat others. You learn how to work with the void through *experiential learning and personal experience*, as you tune into yourself and listen to your personal instructions that come from the divine intelligence inside your body. This wisdom is spoken through visions and feelings, and when the body-mind connection is strengthened, your body communes with you through physical tingles, heat and sensations. You then go out into the world and sense where you are in life through the divine signals around you, that you feel *inside* the body. As we see reflections of self that exist on the inner planes being played out in the external world, we realise that we are literally creating our reality from what's within us. This can be profoundly uplifting or equally scary, depending on our experience Many ancient ideologies and orthodox systems that predated modern religion knew the power of connecting to the Self on the inner planes. However, a lot of this wisdom was driven underground, and unfortunately, some have a vested interest in keeping it buried so they can manipulate the masses. Consequently, our world has become outwardly focused and we've all become unconsciously impacted by our disconnection to the Self. We have, without really knowing it, been brainwashed and programmed to live in a consumer-led world where people on TV become false idols, as we turn away from ourselves and our power. When we turn outwards for happiness, be it to another person, thing, belief, or system, we actually move further and further away from the source of true happiness and all that is sacred in life. When it comes to our relationship with God, the struggle for truth and connection is deeply personal and unique to each individual.

This longing for connection is what leads people back to God.

I can only speak to my truth and share what I have learnt from a place of love in the hope that it might help another, but from my experience, it was my separation from the Self that was the impetus that led me halfway around the world and eventually back home to God within me. You see, I felt so abandoned by God after the years of death and tragedy in my personal life that I felt like part of me had died along the way. I turned this anger into self-enquiry, as I kept questioning why God would do this to me. This blame and shame that I felt inside took me deep into the Christian story, which was how I related to God from my Catholic upbringing. And it was the story of Mary Magdalene, whose role in the early Christian movement seemed to be rather underplayed by the church, that was a major catalyst for my growth and development. As I went down many religious rabbit holes, I discovered a great divide between the various branches of the church which have been squabbling for centuries over what is considered orthodox and authentic scripture and what is thought to be unorthodox. Many early Christian texts, including the Gospels of Mary and Thomas, that were discovered in the Nag Hammadi and The Dead Sea Scrolls in the 40s and 50s, were deemed unorthodox, or Gnostic in nature by the men who were shaping the nascent Catholic Church. Gnostic belief is founded on the principle *that the energy of divinity is in every expression of life, and this divine spark can be liberated through inner wisdom or awareness.* These Gnostic scriptures were excluded from the Canon and erased from the history of Christianity, along with most of the narratives that demonstrated that there is a connection to God on the inner planes via the nous. Since I grew up believing that God was outside and separate from me, this discovery left me feeling like I had been lied to by the church and betrayed at the very core of my being. And so, I travelled the world on my quest for answers, visiting many religious sites and gathering evidence to prove that the church's narrative was wrong. I became so utterly lost in my own righteousness as I searched for 'the truth', without understanding that there is no 'absolute truth'. Truth changes as our consciousness grows and expands, so we can only ever perceive life from where we are, at any given moment in time. And when my consciousness started to expand, I began to see how easily I had misunderstood myself, other people and many aspects of the past in my search to be right. I saw how I judged and condemned others, how I blamed sources outside of me for my unhappiness when I was unable to take responsibility for myself and my feelings. The search for truth became like a game of cat and mouse. I lost myself in other people's dreams on many occasions, but each experience, each journey into the wilderness eventually led me back home, as the niggle inside me connected me deeper to my truth within. And little did I know that the niggle inside would one day lead me to the God spark inside me.

Chapter 8

The Gateway to Creation

—————————— ❖ ——————————

She is the serpent that everyone fears,
for her love is the darkness, her love is the tears.
Be not afraid to step within,
there's nowhere to go, accept to him.

Seek out the places where darkness resides,
shame and guilt, nowhere to hide.
Stillness and compassion, dual aspects of her,
purify my body, let the waters stir.

Poisonous toxins of stories we hold,
burned by the fire turned into gold.
Nestle in the essence of sacred bliss
in the purest way love exists.

As you embark on your spiritual journey into the heart of love, there comes a time when you become acutely aware that the world is designed to help you grow through the dance of opposing forces. Put simply, we've been taught by society to register most of life's experiences and world events as either good or evil, right or wrong, black or white etc...... Our minds are, in general, conditioned by a common code of ethics, and these ethics change and evolve as humanity changes and evolves. For example, the practice of ritualistically sacrificing humans to the Gods was believed to be the highest form of offering by advanced and affluent cultures in ancient times. However, today, the thought of sacrificing a person's life is viewed as a barbaric ritual reserved for only the most ungodly and uncivilised in society – the complete opposite of how the practice was viewed in the past. As humanity walks together through these challenging times of change, we will collectively and individually face many life experiences that will highlight our current beliefs. This will give us an opportunity to reflect and evaluate what works and what doesn't for the good of all going forward. Some of these trials and tribulations may well pull us out of the centre and shake us to the core, but we have to go through them to get to the places where we have unresolved issues. It can be quite destabilising to see the basicness of your being at times, especially when you've been working on yourself for years and think you've got certain traits licked. Spiritual maturity requires daily commitment and lots of practice, so don't be surprised if you find yourself looping around the same old issues time and time again. Looping is part of the process of going deeper so that you can naturally expand into more of who you are. And life in all its glory will keep serving up experiences so that we can perceive ourselves from multiple angles until we've mastered what it is we need to learn. Experiential practices such as yoga, meditation, breathwork and many others are designed to help us with this process. These practices help slow the mind down, creating space inside for us to come out of autopilot and the 'thinking self.' It's only when the mind is tamed that we actually start the process of transcending the dualistic aspect of self and start claiming all aspects of self. And one of the hardest things we will ever have to do when we expand our consciousness is to claim *our own darkness.* Our darkness is the unclaimed shadow that we refuse to see, so we tend to unknowingly project it out into the world, in actions and behaviours that are not part of our true nature. When projection is at play, you are either the light or the dark. The one holding the light is being projected on, and the one doing the projection is doing it because they have some sort of insecurity that they have not seen, and so it has to be played out to be seen. When darkness is unseen and unacknowledged, it tends to make a fuss and plays out as characteristics that we have shamed, blamed, vilified, or suppressed. Behaviours such as lust, greed, lies, anger and hatred are characteristics that we all carry inside, until they are purified, and transmuted into love. Yet, when we are working on our shadow, it is these aspects of self that we get to reclaim and return to the light. If we are able to take a situation and accept that there is an element of truth in what is being said or played out, we can be the light and bring understanding to it. Therefore, we can have a conversation with the other person and work through the issue, and then the projection dissolves, so you don't have to experience it again. If the other person is not willing to do this with you, you can still work on the reflection yourself, and find that part of you that called the situation into being. When dark and light come together, truth is always created. Truth is divinely neutral. Truth just is. Truth does not judge, nor does it try to fix another. In silence, in this space of divine neutrality, something remarkable happens. An opening occurs where our darkness unifies with our light. As we slowly begin to cultivate this presence inside and learn to accept ourselves and others for all that is, it is in this space of divine neutrality that our light naturally dissolves the dark. It takes courage and an open heart to stand in this space and feel love despite the darkness that is there.

When we are working on dissolving density, which is the darkness inside, it can feel like we are being shaken up. Bubbles, waves, or sometimes a whole tsunami of pressure rises to the surface of our being to be released. We know that everything is energy. When there is a lot of chaos in the world, it can feel very unsettling, but how we choose to ride the waves of change is entirely an individual experience. There is in fact tremendous purpose to the chaos, the boat has to be rocked so to speak, so that we can see what is causing the chaos. Energy is foundational and everything in the manifest world comes from the unmanifest world of energy. *Our physical bodies are like 3D prints of our consciousness.* We know that many health issues and diseases have an emotional basis that begins in the ethers, from our thoughts, and is made manifest in the physical. The physical is the final manifestation of the invisible energy created. So, in order to change things, it is much easier to deal with the energy first than the final expression of it in the physical plane. It is much more efficient to go to the root, the core, by working with the invisible and working with the energy. Learning to be energy aware is a skill that we develop as our consciousness expands. If we don't work on our density energetically, we will call on experiences in the physical world to do this for us, forcing us to grow. The darkness can be presented to us in events that can feel highly confrontational, akin to a betrayal, or even aggressive. It can feel like life is giving you a good old slap in the face. These experiences can come as traumatic events or disclosure on the world stage or earth-shattering news in our personal lives. Like when we discover massive cover-ups and corporate corruption by pharmaceutical companies which we rely on for our health. Or, when we find out about the extent of child abuse in the church and we don't want to believe it. Or, we learn that a politician is corrupt and rotten to the core, but we once trusted and voted for the party they represent. Or, maybe a family member that we love and admire cheats people out of money and we feel shamed and confused by their behaviour. There is a whole web of lies and deceit out there that eventually finds you and really shakes you to the core, forcing you to break beyond your limitations and through the cognitive dissonance that we hold in our minds. These things can feel like a form of betrayal, or hardship, or just downright shocking because they challenge our sense of true reality. Cognitive dissonance feels uncomfortable because we can hold two conflicting views in the mind at the same time. For example, if you love to eat hamburgers but you don't want to kill animals for food, this thought will cause discomfort inside. As we evolve individually and collectively and step into a higher way of being, our old behaviours will inevitably no longer align with our new values, and it is this lack of alignment that causes us discomfort. For example, if we've always turned to the medical system and big pharma for our health needs, there will come a time when we have to take responsibility for our bodies and long-term health, rather than thinking a magic pill can do this for us. The same applies to how we govern ourselves, how we share resources, manage finances or educate our kids. It will all come up for review as old systems become outdated and we have to find new ways of living that align with nature's principles of being fair and equitable to all, while not taking from the land and destroying natural resources.

If we do not change our behaviours, we go into denial, and denial of self always involves self-compromise. Self-compromise occurs when you sanction the well-being of another at your own expense or do something that doesn't align with your core truth. When we compromise ourselves for another, be it knowingly or unknowingly, there is always a payoff, a lie we tell ourselves. We try to convince ourselves that what we are doing is for the good of another; otherwise, we would not do it. We often make the greatest compromises for the people we love the most. So, we may do things that do not sit well with us, but convince ourselves we're doing the right thing out of love for our kids, or our family, or partner, when really what we are doing is not standing up for our own needs and loving ourselves. When we self-compromise, we are not self-honouring, and *this denial of self always leads to the compromise of self and others in the long run*, even if there seems to be a temporary win at the time. Self-compromise is a core wound that we all have, and it gets shown to us from the external world through shocking behaviour or events, often from the people we love the most, and it can feel like the rug is being pulled from under you. A classic example is a woman who compromises herself to marry a rich man, only to discover she's really in love with the money and lifestyle and not really her husband, consequently the marriage makes her miserable. Or, a man stays in a job he doesn't really like because the pension is good, but then the firm pulls the plug on the pension, so he feels cheated and let down because he stayed in that job way longer than he wanted and the pot of gold at the end of the line has been taken away from him. Or, we might change our diet believing a certain way of eating is good for us, only to discover it's been harmful to our health and made us sick. There are so many ways we have innocently self-compromised ourselves, so when it plays out in the world, the key to reclaiming your light is to find the wholeness that you are, by integrating the lies, denial and betrayals into your experience. So, when it shows up, in explosive arguments or weird situations, rather than turning on the external 'messenger', pause and turn inwards, look at what is behind the message and what it means for you. This cultivates respect and self-honour within, which is then reflected back to you from the world. As we purify our world within, we get to live in a world where people see the best in each other. This whole process of dislodging the darkness and bringing it to the light can be disconcerting, and lead to you constantly feeling off-centre, thereby, questioning what you're doing, doubting the validity of your relationships, your work, where you live and how you eat. It can bring up layer upon layer of self-doubt, which can make you feel like you are doing everything wrong. But you are not. It's all part of the purification process of dislodging the darkness and cultivating more light within. A natural consequence of releasing the many layers of illusion that were once interwoven into the fabric of our being is that we couldn't tell the lies apart from the truth. We became so uncomfortable in occupying our own space, not connecting to our own consciousness, that it became second nature to be pulled into other people's stories as our energy was harvested in many ways through the distractions of the external world. In our innocence and conditioning, we ended up leading empty lives where we thought we were connected, but often we were living someone else's dream. And as we go through this process to unravel the lies from the truth, it can be quite shocking to see yourself with such luminosity, so try to be kind to yourself and others, remember that we're all in this together and that it's not easy to stand in your authenticity at first. It can feel like you're in limbo, or a transitional zone, like you don't trust yourself, or the world because you are learning to trust from within, in a whole new way. This unknown state of being feels unfathomable at first. It's not pleasurable to feel like you're an outsider in the world. That's because you are observing creation unfolding and you're realising how depleted you are of yourself in the world and so you'll do anything to distract yourself from this discomfort. However, if you allow yourself to stand this ground and go deeper into your presence, you start to acclimate to your presence in the universe. The more you acclimate to yourself, the more awareness you cultivate. The discomfort starts to become more comfortable and you discover that there is a mystery that unfolds, that calls you to be present in your own creation. It is felt within the tingling aliveness of yourself and gives you a childlike wonder as you become consciously aware of your creation in the world, one step at a time. It takes courage to do this, but it is so worthwhile because we get to access parts of ourselves that we couldn't even imagine existed, and this helps us grow and expand exponentially. When we stop fearing pain and discomfort, we start realising we can grow through our challenges and so we stop running away from anything fearful until fear no longer has control over us. When fear no longer has control over us, we stop avoiding anything that causes pain and suffering and realise just how powerful we really are. We realise that we are the ones who are actually painting the picture of our world. We have the power to create, to change the world from the inside out and the source of our wholeness and truth is made manifest when we bring the darkness and light together in union as one. As we keep dissolving the darkness within, we reclaim our light and get to live a higher reality that only a few can imagine. A reality where people see the good in themselves and others, for no other reason than that's all that there is. We just need the willingness to move beyond our existing bandwidth into a higher expression of ourselves. We do this by sitting in our own presence and working through the misunderstandings of our lives with love and forgiveness for all that is. When we work in union with ourselves, we become a beacon of light for others. By holding the presence of our divinity so strongly, we create a ripple of love that emanates into the world for others to see. This ripple sends out an invitation to others to turn inwards and find their own divine connection. When we work on our own darkness and stabilise our own divine presence on Earth, life becomes more effortless for ourselves and others as we allow reality to be as it is, without wanting to fix or change it. The heart works as a gateway for a multi-dimensional self, a personal higher consciousness, to step into your own body to create the new you.

Your heart is the gateway to creation.

We cultivate our source connection by living our lives fearlessly, saying no to our old ways of being as we invite in and stabilise the new. Then, the whole world becomes a divine playgroup where people come and go with lessons that light us up or cause our bodies to shrink and contract. When an experience is expansive, we may feel this growth at a cellular level as energy spinning inside the body. If an experience keeps us small and limited in our expression, we may feel a tightening, stiffening, or contraction inside our bodies. When drama plays out in your world, forgive yourself, learn from it, move from victim to co-creator, and then spend time with yourself to go to the root of the issue And allow yourself the time and space to self-reflect and make the necessary changes so that you don't spew out more negativity into your world. If you go into blame, fear and anger with chaos, you quantum entangle with negativity, and it will only create more and give you a hard time. In times of chaos, try to put more attention into your internal state because that is where every moment starts. It's where you create the next moment and the next and so on. Whatever we feed in a quantum way with our energy, frequency cascades into our reality. In Ancient philosophy, they say that each of us is the only one here, and whilst this seems an impossibility, the world as we know it is way more complicated than we can ever imagine; this analogy is actually part of a conscious realisation that we are the one that is making it all happen.

In a complex multi-dimensional world, which is where we live, there are many different layers of experience that we can reach by changing our frequency. If we want to experience each day as joyous, harmonious, peaceful and fun, we can do so by shifting our frequency to this vibration. It's all possible. What we are actually doing in scientific terms is altering the quantum wave structure, which is something that our ancestors mastered, and something we are all capable of doing too. This means that we can change our physical reality by changing our frequency so that new people and experiences are magnetised into our world. We don't have to go searching for them. We become like a radio dial, knowing that we can only tune into what we are. So, for example, if you dial into hard rock, you'll only hear hard rock. However, if you tune into classical music, this is what you'll receive. It's exactly the same in the universe. Light and love are very high frequencies that dissolve darkness. There's no fight or battle when you hold the field of love, and your struggles are transmuted with ease. The greatest thing you can ever do for yourself is to live your life and allow it to show you the things you should see. The world is designed to give you everything you need to help you learn what you don't understand, but you need to go out into the world and determine what that is. You have to learn by living, by being you and experiencing the richness and fullness of life through everyday living. It is in the little things that we learn to truly master ourselves. Life then shows you where you have misunderstandings in your world and then it's up to you to go inwards and find where your translation of energy is out of alignment.

When two opposing forces come together in the purity of the heart, new life is formed.

We can learn a tremendous amount about ourselves on the spiritual path when we cultivate our sexual energy because this is the energy of creation. Sexuality in its purist sense is the energy that we use to express ourselves in the world. Sexuality is so much more than just genitals and the physical act. We can use this energy to create new physical life, for play and for pleasure. But it can also be used to help us express ourselves in the world and create new forms which we can use it to open our hearts to transform the density that is held inside. When the sexual fire is activated within, the energy can be used for the pure expansion of human consciousness. When a person uses their sexual energy to expand their consciousness or when two people come together with this intention, the magnetic energy they emanate is nothing short of holy. However, most people are completely unaware of the power of sexual energy to transform life and birth new ideas into form. And many of us carry a lot of suppressed shame and guilt around sexual desire, and misuse this primal force which is greatly misunderstood in our modern world. Rather than using our sexual energy to burn out the density inside, we search for others for fulfilment and select partners to balance and harmonise the feelings we have within. Instead of confronting our inner worlds, we turn outwards looking to our partners to distract us from the pain and loneliness inside, thinking that they are the remedy to our feelings of abandonment. But the truth is no one can ever fill this void that we feel inside. And after the initial whirlwind of excitement that comes from new relationships, we start to bring the shame and guilt that we have inside into our relationships. When we relate to another person because we feel unfulfilled in our own lives, we end up bringing all the stories of the past into that relationship. We create and empower a space outside ourselves that constantly needs stimulation when we feel this primal urge bubbling up inside. Because we are not fulfilled and responsible for ourselves, we subconsciously cast a shadow onto others, which slows down our growth and eventually causes chaos in our field. When a woman is in this space and has sexual intercourse, when a man is poking around in the dark, so to speak, if she has not worked on her stuff, all the dross, all the darkness within gets stirred up through the act of lovemaking and is drawn to the surface of her world. The relationship will turn sour very quickly if she is not willing to sit in the discomfort of her creation, turn inwards and find the place inside that needs to change. When we are not conscious of our behaviours and our shadows are at play, a relationship will inevitably fail, with one partner or the other walking away and blaming the other for their behaviour. In these types of relationships, all the 'crap' that we hold onto in life gets stirred up for the other to see. All the jealousy, lies, insecurities and neurotic patterns that we bring to a relationship are brought to the surface for healing, along with the cultural and psychological conditioning and all the fixations and obsessions that have forged our being since childhood and keep us consciously unaware of our true selves. And when we have sexual intercourse, we charge our fields with magnetic energy so we become like magnets, and if we are not strong in our source connection, it will pull you right out. If we are not prepared to see ourselves as a reflection of the other person, then we can easily become repelled by them if they do or say something we don't like. Or, if we value the other more because we believe them to be the one, and greater than ourselves, then we can get pulled into their world and compromise our source connection in the process, which always leads to chaos and resentment in the end. Or, if one partner is prepared to do the work and the other isn't, the relationship becomes fraught and the energies will pull against each other. If we don't learn our lessons, we end up repeating the same mistakes and bring these negative traits to the next partner, as we find ourselves stuck in a never-ending cycle of push and pull. When you are in a conscious connection, you don't need another person in your life to stimulate you because you are already fulfilled inside. Stimulation always leads to some form of distraction or addiction, where we empower something outside ourselves to help us achieve what we can only achieve from within. When we empower something outside ourselves, we move further away from our future potential. The version of ourselves that is outside of time and space, our highest self, has the clearest instructions for our growth, and it is always in front of us. However, when we empower something other than our highest selves, we put that thing in front of our connection to self and disempower ourselves. We no longer get information that is specifically designed for our journey, so we get sidetracked by these relationships. They stifle our creative process and growth, so we don't have the bandwidth or energy to complete the tasks we want to get done because we give all this energy outside of ourselves. However, if we use our sexuality to expand our field, which increases our creative potential, we naturally grow into a higher version of ourselves. And when we are fulfilled in ourselves, we rise up naturally and are magnetised to other people who are also fulfilled within themselves. We don't have to search for other people to make us feel complete, we're already complete within ourselves. We tend to spontaneously meet others who appear in our world because we are vibrating in the same energy field. And when two people are in their creative potential, they have the power to create something which is far greater than they could ever imagine. Their partnership not only serves them but also helps the whole of humanity grow because together they bring in new ideas, concepts and offerings that are literally out of this world, and this allows the world to grow faster.

The secret to conscious connections is for both partners to evolve energetically and find peace in their union and in their ascension. In truth, sacred sexuality is not about the action of intercourse, it is about *the feelings that create the actions* and there are an infinite number of ways to create those feelings through intimate exchanges without actually joining with one another. The more we work with and cultivate our sexual energy, the more we expand our creative potential and then can start to heal naturally - without projecting our crap onto someone else. When a man expands his central channel out and a woman expands her central channel up from the womb they start to rejuvenate and heal the body and have the potential to reach immortality. Conscious connections emerge out of radical self-honesty, where two people are willing to open their hearts to each other and their source, using their union to create a space for elevated consciousness to enter, it then emanates into the collective. When both parties take full responsibility for themselves, the union can be the most powerful catalyst for metaphysical growth. When two people are raw and vulnerable with each other and unafraid to look at their shadow, two become one, and this holy union has incredible potential for humanity.

Golden orbs of essence, two hearts confide,
it's here in truth that creation resides.
The chalice open, drops of nectar pour in,
two became one, woman and him.

Nestling in the stillness, magnetic fields combine,
together as one as the planets align.
A union of souls, journey in the dark,
no space for shadows to leave their ugly mark.

Manifesting in spirit, the noble masculine
A vision bestowed upon me on the Feast of Kings.
The divine nature of Jesus in my Epiphany,
a sudden flash of insight he declares to me:

"I promised I would come, was this not mistook,
time to be of service and write the blessed book.
This story is over, your work is done,
in faith and in trust, no more prodigal son."

From a physical perspective, there are many practices we can do, especially as women, to stabilise our bodies energetically before we enter into a sexual connection with another. The womb is our Earth's brain. The womb translates our reality on Earth and shapes how we communicate with Heaven on the physical plane. Therefore, it is essential that we stabilise our connection to this part of our body because it affects everything we do. If we want to move forward and allow our divinity to come into our body and communicate with us, we have to be able to translate this connection from a clear space. We have to make space inside before we can work with sexual energy. Only when we have a clear open space inside can we paint, write, create and bring through our gifts in this lifetime. However, if a woman has been sexually active, she most likely has a tear etherically and physically in her field and body, which leaks energy from her womb. The energy that is spinning inside the womb starts to drip out and our creative potential leaves us. That's why, as women, many of us feel depleted as mothers, partners and wives, because the truth is we are giving our vital lifeforce away unknowingly. And when we feel depleted inside, we tend to look outside ourselves to be fulfilled, and so we turn to others to fill that gap. So, we look to our kids for joy, our partners for pleasure, our jobs for purpose, when in truth we need to turn inwards, replenish our energy field and make our own happiness the key focus of our lives. This is the reason why when you first enter into a sexual relationship with a new partner your sexual desire tends to go through the roof. It's because intercourse creates a tear in your energetic field and if you don't know how to stabilise your connection, you create this need to be fulfilled, so you need more sex to fill the gap that the sex itself created. This then leads many women into addictive and co-dependent behaviours because they feel so depleted inside. A simple technique to stabilise the body and heal that space is to massage the womb area in a clockwise direction from the left hip bone down to the pubic bone round to the right hip bone and up to the belly button, for 21 cycles or 2 to 3 minutes a day. This will help strengthen the current running through your body, ease period cramps, assist with digestion and help rejuvenate and revitalise the body. You can also work with yoni eggs to strengthen the space so that the current is constantly running or you can place one hand on the heart and one hand on the yoni connecting the two areas with love and forgiveness for all that you are. This can also be extremely energising and healing, especially if you have suffered any trauma in this area. Working with sexual energy helps activate energy in the body, clear out density, strengthen the body and allow us to feel more on a cellular level. When we do this work, we are able to have really open honest communication with ourselves and others, and it is in this space of vulnerability that we magnetise new connections into our world. Our perspective on relationships changes and we choose a partner because we want to work and play with another, not because we need to be with another. This is a major gear shift. It is from this new space that we can expand together naturally, taking personal responsibility for our own sexuality and growth, leaving the lower game of lust behind. These kinds of relationships are not about taking anything from another person; they're about stepping into the unknown aspects of yourself and learning about yourself from your own source connection, using your sexual energy to transform yourself while sharing the experience with another. One of you may be holding space for the other as you raise your consciousness together and expand into a more responsive way of being. When a woman feels safe and surrenders, she opens up a tremendous magnetic vortex at the centre of her womb. This causes her to vibrate and as this happens pathways open up within her and the explosive power of a woman's orgasm, at the same time as the man's, sends tidal waves of energy into the spiritual body, which strengthens it beyond imagination. As this sexual energy moves up the central column, it meets at the crown chakra and a liquid-like substance descends from the left side of the brain, as the feminine side releases red drops into an energetic chalice at the pineal gland. From the right side, white drops are released into the chalice from the masculine. It is the red-and-white essence of the feminine and masculine together that gives us the power to create. Sometimes it will form a new life, and other times we can use it for our own creativity and spiritual awakening. This process of the masculine and feminine elements of our being becoming one also happens at the end of life, as the red and white essence of the mother and father meet at the heart in the inner dissolution of creation. The divine energy of sacred sexuality is the same divine energy of death, both are gateways for creation. This is why an orgasm is sometimes referred to as *la petite mort, the mini death*, as life force or consciousness is expended into the spiritual body and the sensation of orgasm is likened to a mini death.

***

There comes a time on our journey inwards when we reach a certain heart door and know that if we walk through it, we will leave the earthly plane and our physical body. What I want to share with you now is my experience of how this happened to me.

By January 2020, I had moved to Bali for my son's schooling with the intention of making Bali my lasting home. We lived in a beautiful villa in a Balinese compound in the village of Nyuh Kuning, which is in the heart of bustling Ubud, the spiritual centre of the island. I finally felt like I was heading in the right direction, after years of feeling lost and alone. But then Covid came and everything changed again, just like that. As chaos pursued and governments across the world advised their citizens to return home, many foreigners left Bali to travel back to their homelands to be closer to friends and family during those uncertain times. I chose to stay in Bali and watched from afar as the virus spread at alarming rates in the UK and across the Western world. It was hard to comprehend the level of chaos and fear that many of my friends and family experienced during this time in the UK. Bali closed her borders to the outside world and I was locked down on a paradise land and lived in relative peace. It almost felt like I was observing it all from the outside looking in. As the crowded streets of Ubud emptied out, many local people, who had come to rely on tourism for their income, lost their jobs and businesses. But despite the financial difficulties, they showed strength, resilience and kindness to each other and to us foreigners who stayed behind. For me, the Covid pandemic brought with it a new state of being and I saw how people dealt with this new reality in their own unique ways. For many, their lives changed overnight as they were forced to isolate themselves in their homes to prevent the spread of the disease. Children could not attend school, adults could not go to work, restaurants and shops closed and the world as we knew it literally came to a standstill. The whole of humanity had to stop and take stock of their lives for a brief moment. Some people embraced this with an ease and grace that comes from riding the waves of uncertainty and adapting to change. Others simply didn't have the tools to adapt to such drastic changes in their daily lives and focused on the news narrative, which seemed to perpetuate even more fear. I turned to nature and spent my time doing all the things I love. I went to yoga, had lots of massages, pampered myself, met new friends, went to beautiful dinners and took long walks along the Campuhan Ridge. As I honoured myself in this way, my mind relaxed, my body softened and I found myself in a deep state of peace despite the chaos that was growing across the world. But unbeknown to me, I was about to burst out of my Bali bubble and the peace that was transforming me from the inside out.

On March 25th 2020, my life changed forever.

I was staying in a resort on the East Coast of Bali during Nyepi, a festival which marks the start of the New Year, according to the Balinese Saka calendar. Nyepi is a time when the island goes into silent reflection for 24 hours and the Balinese stay at home with family to meditate and set their intentions for the year to come. Many foreigners choose to go to retreats during this time to enjoy the calm solitude whilst in a little more comfort. There were just a handful of other guests staying at the hotel over the 3-day festival. Nobody knew each other, yet we all seemed to be connected somehow. One man in particular was drawn to me like a moth to the flame. It was like our souls knew each other from another time and space. Complete strangers in this life and opposite in every aspect of our being, the magnetic pull between us was extremely strong. Everyone who saw us together witnessed it. We only met 3 times during our 3 days in the grounds of the hotel in the foothills of Mount Agung, yet each time we connected, something truly magical and out of this world occurred. Our first meeting stirred what I can only describe as an Edenic experience where my mind projected me back to the story of Adam and Eve in the Garden of Eden. I found myself in perfect balance in my internal world and felt an unfamiliar force within me beginning to stir. That force was Mother-Earth consciousness, or kundalini energy coming to life. A part of me instinctively knew I was meeting a reflection of myself in this man, from another time and space, to eventually learn something about myself. I know it sounds completely bonkers, but in the infinite possibilities of what is, we exist in parallel lives and worlds, and somehow, I got to experience that with this man. I can only describe the connection between us as nothing short of biblical, and very trippy. Two strangers in a divine play, our souls somehow knew to bring us together to that place in that moment of time. We didn't even need to touch each other physically to spark a cosmic reaction, just being in each other's presence activated us. As we sat on the grass in the hotel gardens on the first evening after dinner, staring up at the stars, our connection opened up his chakras, taking him into a heavenly state where his whole body trembled and vibrated in bliss. I sat and watched in wonder at the effect this energy had on him, but I also knew that we were conduits for something greater than ourselves. The powerful force of nature took him by surprise. He kept looking at me in amazement, asking, "What is this?", as he felt the energy coursing through his whole body. I held him in my presence as his sexual energy activated, and then went back to my room, thinking, wow, this connection is deep. I had never had this effect on another person before, and if truth be known, it felt a bit weird to be so intimately connected to someone whom I had just met – or just met in this lifetime. My mind spun me to sleep, as my intuition knew something weird and wonderful was going on. The next day, he bumped into me by the pool, late in the afternoon, still stunned by what had happened the previous night. He was complaining about stiffness in his neck, so I offered to give him some Reiki. But the second I placed my hands on him, it was like he was taken down into the death realms to a hellish space, which was absolutely terrifying. The experience only lasted a few seconds yet the force between us was so strong it literally scared the life out of us both. He kept screaming at me, "What was that, what the hell was that, what did you do to me?" And all I could say was, "I didn't do anything. You're OK. I didn't do anything." I have never seen another person so petrified in my life. He kept telling me, "I saw the devil, it was the devil"; I just looked at him perplexed, thinking to myself I have absolutely no idea what is going on, but something is definitely up. It took me about an hour to get him to calm down before we went our separate ways. I went back to my room, reeling inside. Neither of us understood what was really going on, I just knew that forces of nature were at play. That evening at dinner, he relayed the tale to the select audience who shared the table with us and I noticed disapproving glances coming my way. To his credit, he didn't once blame me for what had happened although I could see that others around the table were not so approving. He just looked at me and said it was the most amazing life-altering experience of his life. I wasn't feeling quite the same. I was rattled inside and felt like I had somehow inadvertently caused harm to this man. But I also had a feeling that there was more to this man and this story than meets the eye. The third time we met, we sat together enjoying breakfast, when a Mangku, a Balinese Priest, walked out of the temple in the grounds of the hotel all dressed in white robes and blessed us with Holy Water. It was one of those beautiful moments that could only happen in Bali, where you're swept away by the ancient rituals that epitomise the magic and mystery of that sacred island. To me, the blessing felt holy and symbolic of the passing of time. A marker of these times to come, that many prophecies speak to, where 'the meek shall inherit the Earth,' and the world will find peace again. Deep down in the core of my belly, I knew that somehow, we were playing our part in the story of creation, as we did in the beginning and now, we were doing so at the end of times.

When I returned home to my villa in Nyuh Kuning, it was my turn to be activated. I felt an almighty heaviness descend upon me as I entered through the gates of my village as if I was being consumed by darkness. Then, at around 7 pm, while I was doing the dishes, I fell to the floor and had what I can only describe as an in-body death experience, where I returned to the source, and my consciousness collapsed in on me. This experience of 'death' was like falling into a black hole where there was nothing, just me. I returned to my true nature fully aware and stayed inside my body the whole time, and as I did, my consciousness was totally transformed or upgraded, if you like. This falling into myself took about 20 minutes and I was completely aware of the entire experience; at one point on the journey within, I came to an inner 'doorway', which I can only describe as the point of no return. It was the point at which I could choose whether to stay in my body or go. If I had chosen to leave, I would have passed on, and my time on Earth would have been over. I knew this instinctively. The awareness that I could pass over, just like that, consciously, stunned me at the time. I kept thinking about my young son and my daughter, and my own life, and I kept saying, "No, no I'm not leaving now, I've not come this far only to leave. How dare you do this to me!" I had a few choice words with God, who was not upstairs in some imaginary heaven of my childhood mind but was inside of me. There were a lot of tears and shock and some pleading for my life. I was very scared, terrified in fact, because I knew this was the end. Once the initial panic subsided, I took a few deep breaths and steadied myself. I realised I was still alive. I cried like a baby, as I understood the enormity of what I was experiencing. I was experiencing death, if you like, or the void, or the space in between, whatever you choose to call it. It was a living consciousness inside my body. I felt like I was nothing and everything, like the entire universe had collapsed inside of me. All I kept saying to myself was, "It's all me. It's all me." I was able to acknowledge what was happening to me and that I could die at that moment if I opened that door, and that I was being gifted with the choice. I liken the experience to an old shaman who knows it's his time, going out into the desert to turn his life off, just like that, with ease and grace, but it's fair to say my experience was not graceful at all. But I chose to stay and, after a lot more crying and self-realisation that it was all me, I managed to pull myself together as I returned to calmness. I spent the next two weeks going to see an acupuncturist to help ground me, as I could not get my head around what had happened to me. I felt like I was going mad, as I couldn't quite work out what was real and what was my imagination. I kept searching for answers outside because I wanted to know what had happened to me, and in hindsight, that was a big mistake. All I kept thinking was, "OMG it's all me, and the world out there is not what I thought it was." I had what you might call a red pill Matrix moment, where I broke out of my own ignorance and started to face the painful truth of my own reality.

Approximately two weeks after this black hole event, I sat bolt upright in the middle of the night and felt a drop of oil pour down inside my head as I tasted this oily substance at the back of my throat. In Eastern traditions, this oil is called Amrita, which means overcoming death. I tried to speak to people about my experience at the time, to get some support and to make sure I hadn't gone totally mad, but I just got a lot of blank faces. I have met few people who really understand this phenomenon and even fewer who have experienced it. If truth be told, I didn't really understand it myself until I started to rewrite this book and discovered the significance of the union between light and dark, which is what creates the truth within.

Whenever these mystical crazy things happen to me, which they do all the time, I try to seek understanding, often through others; I think that's a very human thing to do, but I've since realised that this was the whole point: I was being taught a lesson in sovereignty, which is part of the process a person has to go through in order to embody their divinity and what I had to do was to start relying on my own innate understanding of life and stop searching outside of myself for answers. What I now understand is that I experienced the death of the false self and a rebirth of my true nature within. What I mean by false self is the illusion that I am not responsible for my own life. I had stepped into a space where I was now able to take personal responsibility for myself. And this is massive because it completely changed the way I perceived reality. I now had the awareness to see, and so I could choose whether or not to blame others for how I was feeling inside. I had given so much of my power away to others, to my children, family, partners, friends, to anyone who ever really came into my path, I was very willing to devolve my power as part of my co-dependent tendency, but now it was time to take it back and to take full responsibility for my actions, thoughts and deeds. I had, if you like, expanded my heart to a point where I pierced the veil of consciousnesses within and touched upon God, deep within me.

Experiencing the 'death' of the false self, helped me overcome many of my inner fears. I had to face all of my limiting beliefs and see where I was still holding onto old stories of lack, or it forced me into positions where I could see where I wasn't loving towards myself or others. It brought forth all the unconscious shadows that I carried around into play, using the activated sexual energy to transmute the misunderstandings of my life into love. It was as if for the first time in my life I was no longer afraid to be me, warts and all. I could embody a level of presence that connected me to everyone and everything around me, and this new level of awareness blew me away. There was a six-month period of adjustment after I fell into the black hole when I felt very destabilised and very much alone as I adjusted to the world outside of me. I had to do a lot of grounding and bring myself back down to Earth as I literally tried to pull aspects of myself back into my body. Prior to this, I had a tendency to want to leave my body, escape myself, but I knew I had to bring this awareness in and embody it. I was, if you like, using this light of God to fill myself up and to clear the density out of my body. Bringing Mother-Earth consciousness together with the light of God inside of me, creating Heaven and Earth within. It was very hard to navigate; I thought I was going to die many times over as I went down many rabbit holes while trying to make sense of life with this newfound awareness inside of me. I was going through the second stage of the awakening process. I had already awakened to the light in me some years earlier and now I was awakening to the dark in me, the other side of life that I did not want to see. And this brought me to my knees, as I saw what humans were capable of doing to each other. True reality had opened my eyes to a lot of ugliness, which I had to learn to accept for what it was, even the dreadful unthinkable things in this life. The man who activated my kundalini represented darkness: a wolf in sheep's clothing, he came into my experience to allow me to see my own darkness within so that I could transmute it into light. He was not a man I would ever want to meet again, yet somehow through it all, I didn't feel hatred towards him, or people like him. This experience helped me understand that if I am connected to all things, then I too must be capable of all things, including being the worst of society, maybe not in this lifetime but in another. And the newfound awareness that I was cultivating within profoundly changed the way I judged others, helping me reach a state of deep acceptance for all of life, including the parts that I didn't want to see. The pure love and compassion I felt inside, not just for myself but for all humanity, including him, overwhelmed me at times.

As the sexual energy transformed my physical, emotional, spiritual, and mental bodies, I remember saying to myself repeatedly "OMG it's all real. It's all real." By which I mean, the unseen world is real. In fact, the unseen world makes up 97% of our reality, and through opening my heart to life, I started to see more and more of it. I was developing what the ancient philosophers called "eyes that could see," which is an awakening of the third eye. And my physical eyes adjusted as my dimensional sight came online; my vision blurred many times as my eyes adjusted to my new world. In fact, all my senses became heightened. The air became crisper, the trees looked greener, the oceans seemed to sparkle again and I sensed a renewed vitality returning to the land. I also started to emanate a glow that came from within, and the people in Bali could feel my presence around me. I was changing within and my world was changing too.

Acceptance is what got me through this challenging time in my life because it was not easy. Acceptance is the key to cultivating the level of forgiveness in everyday life that is needed to comprehend such a huge shift in consciousness. It took me two years to stabilise this new awareness in my field before I returned to the UK to start a new chapter in my life. I arrived on the Spring Equinox, which felt like a poignant time to end my journey through the darkness into the light. I had come full circle, back home to my Self to be reunited with my family and friends and the people whom I loved most in the world. When I landed in the UK, everything felt familiar yet different. In many ways, I didn't 'recognise' this new me I had become. I felt out of alignment with the energy around me and had to adjust to the new rhythms in the West.

Despite years of working on myself, returning home seemed to trigger many old niggly childhood insecurities that I thought I had dealt with. And that kind of ruffled my feathers for a while. I felt like I was starting again and the truth is, I was. But this time I had the tools to face myself with a little more grace and wisdom.

Chapter 9

You Are the Way

———————————— ❖ ————————————

We are living through a moment in time where our beautiful world is rapidly changing and we are being called to change as well. Although this may look and feel chaotic right now, what we are experiencing, is in fact a force for good. As people start to galvanise and support each other, the impact of our collective thoughts, actions and feelings will have a ripple effect on the world. And this ripple effect will change the way we live. It will change the way we think about ourselves and others, the way we work, how we educate our kids, how we spend our money and how we treat our bodies. As the ground beneath us shifts and stirs we will be faced with our own personal challenges. How we deal with these challenges really depends on how well we know ourselves and how willing we are to sit in the fire of uncertainty and connect deeply to our truth. This connection to our true nature is what allows us to prosper and thrive because the more we connect to ourselves, the more of ourselves we become. Nobody can make this connection to you. *You are the way.*

To move forward in life, we have to stop our old ways of being and turn inwards. When we turn inwards, we discover who we truly are. This journey inwards is a process of purifying the mind to open the heart. We open our hearts when we let go of the beliefs and stories, identities and attachments that keep us tied to the past or focused on a future that will never come. When we live in the heart, we can only ever be in the here and now, which is where the real magic lies. As our heart slowly opens, our body-mind connection comes back online, we start to transform on a cellular level and heal from within. The opening of the heart invites us to be brutally honest with our lives and calls for radical authenticity, as we get to meet ourselves in the purity and innocence of this sacred space. So how do we turn inwards? Well, we all have our own unique way of being. You don't have to be 'spiritual' to connect with yourself. You just have to be good and do what makes you feel complete inside, in your daily life. Put simply, you just have to live and do what you love doing, which is being kind to yourself, to the Earth and to others. You are in truth connected all the time, but you're just not aware of it. So, when you're spending time being creative: painting, writing, or dancing, if you're pumping iron at the gym or walking in nature, playing a musical instrument, baking cakes, or making love, just take a moment to acknowledge yourself in these activities. when you find yourself there, in every moment, the joy and appreciation for life grows. We are all capable of finding our true selves if we dare to live our lives as nature intended. We do this by doing good, being good, committing to ourselves and having fun. We learn by living, by making mistakes and by finding out what does and doesn't work for us. Most of the challenging experiences that happen in life occur because a core wound from our childhood is calling to be seen. All the trauma, beliefs and conditioning from the past are stored as energy in a field that surrounds us, and it speaks back to us through the experiences that come into our world. Energy is not typically something we see, rather energy is something we feel. If we want to understand who we are, we need to be able to feel energy as it bubbles up inside of us and learn how to align with it. When we get authentic and feel what is real, we naturally discharge the energy, but this requires commitment and refinement of the Self, which we learn by being out in the world and being willing to make mistakes and taking personal responsibility for ourselves. *Feelings speak louder than words.* The problem is, more often than not, we are completely unconscious of how we feel and totally out of alignment with the energy in our field. We might say things like, "Oh I'm fine" when really, we are reeling from pain inside. But when we open our hearts, we allow ourselves to feel the truth, and the truth never lies. So if we feel pain, anger, rawness, or sadness inside, we are feeling it because it is there, it is real, and it is ours to deal with. It doesn't matter what external situation triggered the feeling inside of you, the person who is feeling it is you, you were just unconscious of it before. We live in a world of constant distraction, where everything is designed to take our attention away from ourselves and our feelings. Therefore, finding the time to go inwards requires real discipline and commitment to self. Refining ourselves is a lifelong journey. When we are present and conscious of our behaviour in the world, we begin to take responsibility for our lives. We no longer play the victim, blaming or shaming others for how we feel, and this is both liberating and challenging at the same time. It can bring up many memories that we thought we had dealt with and activate feelings of lack inside, which often take us by surprise. The key to navigating these times is to be deeply compassionate to yourself, whilst remaining open to the wonders of what is. But when we align what we are feeling (heart) with what we are saying (mind), we begin to discharge the feelings organically. By bringing our words and feelings into harmonious union, we allow pain to pass through us, without attaching any story to it. And then the pain goes away. As we become brave and move through our pain, life becomes sweeter, simpler and more enjoyable.

When we are anchored into ourselves, we grow stronger. The only person who can connect to the true you is you, and there is no better time to do this than today. This book is designed to help with this process. It will call you deep within and ask you to go beyond your existing beliefs to see a perspective that is not your own. When we do this, we can learn a lot about ourselves by feeling whether something resonates with us or if it triggers the hell out of us. If my words trigger you, then pause for a moment and ask yourself why. Find the part of you that is being pushed on, and explore how it is making you feel. Then, pause and let the feeling go and know that you have grown a little stronger because of it.

Your connection to your heart frees you from suffering. Your light frees you from ever needing someone or something outside yourself to make you happy. Freedom is found when we are willing to be authentic and say no when society is screaming yes and this takes courage in the beginning. When you are willing to face your fears and all the conditioning that keeps you small, a new you emerges from the ashes of the past and is so much more than you could ever imagine. The old you will be swept away by the tides of your own being, as nature calls back her own to be reinvented and sent back into the world. To be reborn and recreated often. Like a cosmic Pac- Man pulling in all the bits of the self to be reclaimed and repackaged as something new. Once you connect to your true nature, you further recreate yourself from the seeds of your personal instruction time and time again. Always growing. Ever expanding into more of who you are.

Your inner guidance is tailored to you. If you are unsure about something in life, always ask yourself the question first, before you turn to others. You have the perfect answer inside, you just have to be willing to find it. If you take the time to ask yourself first, you will start to cultivate more trust in your own inner guidance and this will grow and blossom over time. If you can't find your own solution, then it can be helpful to turn to other sources. But when you do, always re-source this information and make it your own. Apply it to your life through your own lens. Take what resonates and leave the rest behind. In this way, you empower yourself and continue to grow through your own source connection.

Find your guiding principles and live by them. After writing my books, I created "10 Ways to Live in Divine Union", a template to help me understand myself and the world I'm in. I invite you to take 5 minutes as you read this concluding part of the book to reflect on each concept and think about how they apply to you, and perhaps consider making your own.

10 Ways to Live in Divine Union

1. Sit in silence and hear the sound of the soul, listen to the one who is in control.
2. Let your heart be your guide the wisdom of the universe is inside.
3. Be the best that you can be for it is only in the moment that we truly see.
4. I am outside looking in, life is an illusion, there is no sin.
5. You are a ripple in the universe, creating each moment for better or worse.
6. Your purpose on Earth is to love without remorse and to bring this wisdom back to source.
7. Hidden behind the stories we tell, is a magical love and it's under your spell.
8. The alchemy of suffering is not what it seems, it's an invitation to step into the heart and live your dreams.
9. Judge not by right or wrong, let love be the essence in every song.
10. Truth cannot be known; it is ever-changing and not ours to own.

1. Sit in silence and hear the sound of your soul, listen to the one who is in control.

Silence has its own way of being. It leads you to a space within where everything you ever wanted is waiting patiently for you. This inner world feels rich and alive and every person on Earth has something amazing inside that wants to be brought into life. The stream of creation lives in every moment of silence where we connect to ourselves. It doesn't speak in words but in energy and feelings. When you step into this stream and connect to yourself, the path ahead lights up, and with this awareness, you can create the best life imaginable, knowing that the right people and resources will come your way if you follow your heart and act from the guidance that comes from within. This takes courage, commitment and clear sight and at times it will make no sense and you will feel like your whole world is turning inside out, and in many ways, it is, because we are learning how to live in union with life again. This is a huge change to how most people live. We currently live as consumers of reality, where we tend to follow the will of others, without even realising that we are doing this. This leads to us being dissatisfied with our lives, blaming the world for our problems, when in fact it is our disconnection from our own lives that creates the problems that we experience in the world. One moment of silence builds on another . The simple act of silence is all that it takes to change your life forever because once you have seen the truth inside, you can never turn back, and the beautiful unveiling of life begins from this one perfect moment.

2. Let your heart be your guide, the wisdom of the universe is inside.

As your lifeforce comes online, your heart starts to communicate through the language of feelings inside your body. You start to stream information from the universe, which comes from your highest self, through the heart, which are your personal instructions on what to do next. You unpackage these instructions inside your body, interpreting the wisdom from the universe through visions, feelings, intuition and clear knowing. You then take this wisdom out into the world and create your reality from the inside out. By coming back to silence you allow the heart to find the way. The heart is connected to the entire universe and beyond, so life unveils itself in the purest, most efficient and perfect way for you if you follow the way of the heart. To do this you have to drop out of autopilot and start critically thinking for yourself, which requires true authenticity. It takes bravery, raw honesty and personal responsibility to follow the heart, especially if you have spent your entire life conforming to society's ways. However, conforming actually takes away your personal freedoms and disempowers you because you stop asking why am I doing something and carry on doing things that frankly make no sense. The desire to conform comes from the basic human need to feel safe. We have created the notion of safety by wrapping ourselves up in beliefs and structures, based on common values in a consumer reality. But as we strengthen our own source connection, we realise that the universe is supporting us from within. We are safe and held in love by life itself.

3. Be the best that you can be for it is only in the moment that we truly see.

This process of turning inwards asks you to be willing to be your best. Nothing more, nothing less. Being your best is about allowing whatever needs to be seen to come to the surface of your reality, however challenging it might be. Some days our best might be curling up in a corner and crying, and that's OK. When we stay open to all of life, we don't resist, deny, or suppress what is there, and this creates a space for healing to occur. In the timelessness of the present, life can flow through us effortlessly. This means we actually have to get out of our own way and let life in, which is all about letting go of control and stepping into faith. If we allow life to flow through us, we can change effortlessly and all the patterns and beliefs we hold onto will come to us, in perfect timing, through the story of our lives. If we can be our best and live from one moment to the next, doing the next right thing and dealing with all that is in front of us, then we will flow through these changing times with ease *because the path of least resistance is the one directly in front of you.* The path of least resistance is designed perfectly for you, by the highest version of you who has already mastered life. When we are present in our lives, we are in tune with the subtleties of the world we live in. But the truth is, we actually have everything we need within ourselves to live in harmony with the world. It is all available to us, we just need to be willing to see it. That means we must be willing to see the things we need to change and be that change when it comes our way. We do this by slowing down and paying attention to how we feel inside. When you feel yourself being pulled by life, stop and ask yourself, what inside of me is resisting the experience that is right in front of me? Then, take a moment to breathe into that feeling. Let it be and have faith that the silence within will do its thing. Then, act on what you discover about yourself. As you practise being present, you start to refine what it feels like to be you again and you start to discover which experiences feel good for you and which ones no longer do.

4. I am outside looking in, life is an illusion, there is no sin.

As we learn to see clearly, we begin to experience life in the moment from an objective perspective. *We become the observers of ourselves in our lives,* and this is a major milestone and something to celebrate because life gets easier from here on in. When you can observe yourself in your life, you tend not to react so strongly to things outside of yourself because you start to see life from multiple perspectives. You get to see the detail and parts of the bigger picture play out at the same time and this helps us understand and accept life for what it is, without resisting, denying, blaming, shaming, or avoiding our part in the story. This allows you to meet your old patterns, traumas, beliefs, philosophies and memories, with more understanding and ease for what they are. They are tools to assist you in becoming more of who you are. And it is from this observer state that we get to reconcile our connection to God and some of the fundamental beliefs that we may have about creation and original sin. And this can challenge how you perceive the role of Religion in the world going forward. The 'I am' is the ascended mastery of you, the you that is outside time and space, your divinity, connecting with the you that is inside time and space, it is the you that is here now. One day, the two will become one.

A way to imagine this concept is to open your hands in front of the heart shoulder-width apart.

Imagine that the left palm is your divinity and your right palm is you in human form.

Now feel the distance and the space between the palms of your hands. When we expand consciousness inside our bodies, we begin to bring the higher version of ourselves into our bodies.

As you imagine this, start to bring the palms of your hands closer and closer together, and feel the sensations and connection to your divinity grow stronger as you bridge the gap between you inside time and space and your infinite nature outside.

Now bring your palms together so that the two meet in prayer at the heart

Now feel the power of this connection.

Feel the potential in the palms of your hand.

5. You are a ripple in the universe, creating each moment for better or worse.

When enough people start doing things differently, the world around them radically changes, and this creates a ripple on the global stage that is felt by all. And as this ripple grows, as more people feel the call to change, a seismic shift in consciousness occurs and we stop and question why we do things that no longer serve our highest good. However, as we start to turn inwards and make changes in our lives, the pressure to change creates the necessary force needed to change, because without the pressure, we would do nothing. Of course, this may bring about a feeling of instability, we can feel a little out of control, and we may perhaps want to hide under a rock and ignore what is coming up for us. And that's OK. We all go through these times of uncertainty when we just don't want to deal with our stuff, but eventually, the pressure builds up inside to a point where we can no longer avoid ourselves, and when this happens, we start to understand that we are the force behind this seismic shift in consciousness that is causing us to change. Through our desire to make the world a better place, we are individually and collectively being the change we want to see in the world. We are all going through this beautiful and powerful experience in our own unique way.

As we connect to our inner worlds, the outside world starts to become alive. We get glimpses of what could be and experience monumental mic drop moments when we see creation in all its wonder and start to finally understand that everything counts and that we are, in fact, a ripple in a vast universe of our own making. This is a huge discovery for most people, as it takes us out of the mind and into a space of personal responsibility, where we finally understand that we are making everything happen in our world, by our own thoughts and actions. Our worldview shifts as our expanded awareness brings us to a state of acceptance of what is. Our belief structure evolves in the following way:

> life is happening to me
> life is happening for me
> life is happening though me
> life is

6. *Your purpose on Earth is to love without remorse and to bring this wisdom back to source.*

It is fair to say that there are many misconceptions about what love is and for many the search for love is the ultimate journey into the unknown. When you search for love in the eyes of another, in material things, or in anything outside yourself, you may find a temporary quenching for love, but it never lasts because pure love can only ever be nurtured from within. Pure love is not something we can ever find outside of ourselves. Pure love is our source of power, and like a battery, we need to be charged. We power up by taking the time to connect to ourselves each day. It's very simple. The more time you spend connected to the source, the stronger your charge becomes. And when you go out into the world and create from this place of pure love, you align with the highest life for you. This is when big life-changing events occur. You may suddenly find the courage to do things you never thought you'd do. People begin to move in and out of your world, and new opportunities come your way, helping you achieve your dreams.

As we become less attached to outcomes and open to the infinite possibilities of life itself, we free ourselves from trying to control life, and say to ourselves, 'OK, show me, what next?' As our faith in the universe grows, we discover that everything we ever need is right in front of us. When we stop competing with ourselves and others, and relax more, life becomes extremely peaceful, and we start to enjoy the simple pleasures in life again and become very content in our own world, regardless of where we are or what our situation is. When we relax into life, we don't take ourselves too seriously. We can laugh at our mistakes and there is an innocence to us again, and a willingness to take more risks because we're not afraid of getting things wrong. We become almost childlike again in our curiosity about life, but we also have the wisdom and grace of time behind us. We become more careful with our words, our thoughts and our actions because we understand that we are connected to everything, and this makes us more caring and mindful of our own bodies and how we live on Earth. And when we finally understand that we are making it all happen, we change our lives forever, and from that point on, we fine-tune ourselves so that we live more harmoniously with our world.

7. Hidden behind the stories we tell, is a magical love and it's under your spell.

Stories are useful tools that have been passed down to us throughout the ages to help us unlock different aspects of our being. As we evolve as souls and our connection to the divine deepens, stories start to resonate deeply on a subconscious level, which is why people relate to storytelling so easily. Because stories resonate so deeply at a soul level, when one person dares to share their story as I've done through my books, the stories act as a conduit for healing for others. But it is not the story itself that matters, it's the energy behind the words that count. As we become more energetically sensitive, we start to feel the energy behind the words written or spoken. This means we have the ability to feel the intention of another person regardless of what they are actually saying or writing. And that ability to feel energy allows us to discern if a person is being genuine or not, despite what they are saying. As we become more energy aware, we will be able to decipher what is false, what is fear-based, what is being said in defence, which words have an underlying energy of control and what is being said from pure love. As we become more energy aware nothing is unseen.

Stories are often memories from the past with which we identify. As we practice sitting in silence, we start to notice certain stories we keep telling ourselves that keep us locked inside our limited minds and looping in a cycle of perpetual disconnection from our infinite potential. Yet as we connect more deeply to the source, we come to a point where the mind can no longer process the amount of information flooding through our bodies and we kind of short-circuit the mind, which sounds ominous, but what it does is liberate us from the restrictions that we put on ourselves. So, we collapse all the stories of the past into us, as everything converges into the point of singularity and we emerge from the other side as we move beyond the programmes of the mind. The heart then becomes the main driving force behind our reality, as we free our minds and begin to clear up the misunderstandings of our life from this new space of love inside the heart.

8. The alchemy of suffering is not what it seems, it's an invitation to step into the heart and live your dreams.

The suffering and trauma that most people experience in life has served to get us to where we are now. But we cannot carry it with us. Once the mind is free, we cannot ignore the suffering inside because the pressure it creates is too great, so we have to actively clear anything that is causing suffering in our world from our field. We do that by moving through our pain not avoiding it, then alchemising the pain, using it to create more space inside. Depending on how invested we are in our old ways of being, we can evolve through this process with ease or not. The choice is ours. And it is a choice.

To break the pattern of suffering, we have to connect with ourselves daily and sit in silence. You can do this in many ways, but just being present with yourself and taking 5-10 minutes in the morning and before you go to sleep is all it takes. Bathe yourself in the silence and allow it to vibrate through every cell of your body.

Next, be willing to sit with the uncertainty and really take the time to feel what's going on inside. Sometimes it helps to write it out as a stream of unconscious ramblings. Writing helps bring feelings to the surface, and seeing them on paper is often enough to process what's going on inside.

Taking responsibility for everything you say, do, feel and think helps you see the unconscious patterns that keep repeating in your world. When you see your part in it all, it helps you consciously change your behaviours and create new ones. Deep beliefs hold on tight, so you have to learn great humility and forgiveness to get to the root of your core issues.

Criticism gets you nowhere. So often, we criticise ourselves without even knowing it. We say things like oh my hair is horrible today, or I'm fat, or I'm not clever and this reinforces negative patterns of lack within our system. We have to stop doing this.

Comparing yourself to others is also pointless. You're wired to be you, not someone else. Therefore, if you gauge your success or failure against someone else's template, you will never be happy. It's like comparing apples with pears, it just doesn't work. Your job is to help you.

Judging yourself or others only perpetuates more judgement. Judging yourself is just another form of criticism or comparison. And you have no right to judge others because you're not walking in their shoes so you have no idea what lessons they need to learn. That's their stuff. Let them have it. You have enough of our own stuff to deal with.

Stop trying to control life. Most people are way more controlling than they realise, so when you find yourself pushing up against life don't beat yourself up. Catch it. See it. Feel it. Then let it go.

9. Judge not by right or wrong, let love be the essence in every song

As we create our lives on the foundations of freedom from within, we begin to see how we actually consciously choose how we live from one moment to the next. Our truth is ours alone, and because we have embodied this understanding, we don't need to be right or prove others wrong. Everything is perfect as it is, and this in itself is incredibly humbling. It frees us from the analytical mind, which often sees life through a bipolar lens of 'good or bad, right or wrong', 'like or dislike.' When we do this, we judge life, rather than just experiencing what is there. There is a subtle but important difference If we observe a situation from a divine neutral perspective and not voice a judgement either way, we avoid potential conflict with ourselves and others. This is because we never really know, how a person is going to respond to our opinion because we are coming from our perspective and not theirs.

However, if we connect to ourselves energetically and engage in conscious conversations with ourselves and others, our body is activated energetically and we can feel the energy inside as tingles or flushes of heat or bubbling gas as we connect. It is the energy behind the words that counts. We can take another person's perspective into our field, and re-source it for our own growth and expansion, even if we don't agree with it. If something comes into our field that we don't resonate with, we allow it to pass through us rather than attaching anything to it which would cause disharmony within. When we are in divine neutrality in this way, we don't judge ourselves or others. We allow the energy to speak, and energy just is. We don't attach to it, hold on to it, or analyse it. We experience it in the moment and then allow it to pass through us naturally. In this way, as energetic beings, we keep unfolding, knowing that there is no right or wrong, just life in all its imperfect perfectness.

Most of the time, we can show our strength through our silence. It's the intensity of the words that counts, not the volume of words. When you speak from the heart, and fill your own space, no one else can command it, only you. High vibrational people don't actually need to say anything to make their presence known, in truth nothing needs to be said or done. Pure love is so genuine, it can be felt from afar.

10.*Truth cannot be known; it is ever-changing and not ours to own.*

There is no absolute truth. We are constantly moving, expanding, rising and changing. We cannot hold onto anything in the end. That means we must be prepared to let go of the fundamental truths that shape our lives and this can be extremely challenging at times. As we pioneer a new way of being individually and collectively, as we build this new world together, everything we ever believed in will change. We must find courage deep within to face these uncertain times. Uncertainty and change speak to life itself. There will be moments when life is stable, when we think we've got it all sussed out, and then, something unexpected happens. Life throws us a curve ball, and we're in chaos again, all shaken up. The dance between order and chaos is the true nature of reality. How we deal with it is the master's journey. We can meet life with grace and ease or we can be fearful. We always have a choice.

As we evolve through new sectors of consciousness and embody higher perspectives of reality, we discover new layers of truth, which may challenge our sense of being or even bring us to our knees. This can send us spinning off-centre and destabilise us, pulling us out of our heart-based core. The best way to ride these waves of change is to focus your energy on what's happening in front of you. This pulls you back into the heart, into the timelessness of now, and out of overwhelm.

As we experience ourselves out in the world, our sense of knowing becomes true wisdom when we apply what we have learnt on the inner planes to everyday life. Truth feels easy and uncomplicated. If we come across something in life that does not feel simple and right, then it's probably not. We have to go out, live and have faith in ourselves, even if we have no idea what we're doing. It's this willingness to try that propels us forward. When doubt creeps in, which is will, we tend to go into the analytical mind and question everything. That's when life gets tricky. If we look outside ourselves for solutions or distractions rather than turning inwards and relying on our own intuition, things get more complicated. The problem is that sometimes when we desire something so badly, and our intuition tells us we've got it wrong, we can get stuck in a battle between heart and mind. And the mind can be very convincing. Yet deep down inside, we do know what we have to do to improve our lives, whether it's a change of mindset or lifestyle or both, but somehow, we get stuck in this merry-go-round of repeating the same patterns time and time again, and we make all sorts of excuses. But ultimately it is only us that can make the changes in our lives.

Afterword

Letter to Self: Written in Bali, March 2020

You are living in unprecedented times of change and it may appear that the world 'out there' is falling apart, and in many ways, it is. These changes you see on the global stage are in fact a product of changes that have already happened inside you because you choose to see life in another way. You dreamed of creating a world that is free and equal for all. These dreams are slowly becoming a reality, and as you break free from the systems that have held you down for thousands of years, it creates an opportunity for everyone to break free. If you want to free yourself from the shackles of corruption and injustice that have plagued the world for so long, you need to reclaim your sovereignty. You do this by changing your world from the inside out. As changes occur on the inner planes, you will start to take responsibility for yourself and begin to see that you created everything in your life, perfectly just as it is. Once you realise that you are actually co-creating your reality with the divine, you will start to play, have fun and experience life for all its infinite potential. Even with this level of awareness, you will still meet challenges, this is just the nature of reality, however, there is no need to suffer through the difficult times as you have done in the past, and I hope you find peace in this knowing. As your consciousness evolves, your life will never be the same again and you will learn to accept this with grace and appreciation for all that you have learnt. You will find yourself no longer believing in 'facts' that you once knew as truth, and you might find letting go of these beliefs to be a struggle if you remain attached to a particular way of thinking. Be gentle to yourself, you didn't know what you didn't know, and as you evolve, you will start to see things from a higher perspective that was not available to you before. This evolution of humanity is happening naturally, there is nothing to do as such, other than be fully present in your own experience. You will start to experience energy moving inside your body. This energy is life itself and it carries a divine intelligence that is your own source connection designed to guide you one step at a time. No one is given more than they can handle, so there is nothing to fear. You will go through this process in your own unique way, and I AM always by your side. You will hear me as the quiet whisper of your soul, and whenever you search for me, you will find me. I encourage you with all heart to find and nurture your own path. You created these

to help guide you at this time because you always knew this change was coming. These teachings build on each other, and whenever you find yourself out of connection, confused, in doubt or losing faith in life, they will help bring you back home to the guiding light inside you, for I Am you, and you are I, and together we are one. Remain true to yourself and never forget, YOU ARE THE WAY.

Thank you for being here,

Big Love, as always,

Dee xxx

Acknowledgements

I would like to express my heartfelt gratitude to all the people who have loved and supported me over the years.

To my children Millie and Fionn for being bright lights in my world.

To my Mother and Father who taught me resilience and what it means to be family.

To my brothers and sisters. For allowing me to be the 'good' one in the gang. I hope I played my role well.

To Tony, Martyn and Paul. The men in my life who loved and helped me become the woman I am today.

To my Besties, Debbie, Natalie, Sharon, Angela, Anna, Laura and Vanessa. For always being there, You are my rocks.

To my Soulsisters Alex, Jennifer, and Taran for all the crazy woo woo conversations, and moon rituals. The Magic works.

To Danielle Wrate for being the first person to pick up my story and for helping me bring it to life. Thank you for believing in me.

To Rev. Ariel Patricia for reminding me that it is my own story that really counts.

To Patricia Frida, who created the new artwork for the re-edits. They are divine.

To Greg Scott and his badass editing skills. And for being a mentor to my son.

To all the spiritual warriors, too many to mention, living their best lives and helping humanity along the way. Together we've got this.

About the Author

Dee Delaney was born in the UK to Irish parents and lived in India and Southeast Asia for over 10 years. She developed a profound love for the East from an early age, and she is extremely sensitive to the injustices in the world, especially when it comes to disadvantaged women and children. Dee had worked at the BBC for many years when her husband, Tony, died suddenly while doing a charity mountain climb. His death, along with the subsequent deaths of two former partners, her father and a best friend changed her perspective on life, and in 2016, she embarked on a seven-year spiritual quest, swapping her charmed life in the West for a simpler existence in Goa and then Bali. As a result of this journey of self-discovery, she wrote a trilogy of books called *The Truth is Within*, and her writing is ingrained with the insights she gained during her spiritual odyssey. Dee has now returned to the UK to be close to friends and family, and when she's not travelling, she works as a spiritual coach helping others to connect to their divinity within.

To discover more visit www.deedelaney.co.uk or join her community on Facebook and Instagram @deedelaney01

About the books

My Journey to the Other Side
(Book 1 in *The Truth is Within* trilogy)
Exploring Everyday Spirituality

By the age of 41, Dee was the woman who 'had it all' – a loving partner, a family, a successful career and plenty of money. But just when it seemed things couldn't get any better, her beloved husband, Tony, an outwardly fit and healthy man in his early forties, died of a sudden heart attack while doing a charity mountain climb, leaving Dee widowed and a single mum to their two-year-old son and a teenage daughter from a previous relationship. A series of further tragic events followed, compounding Dee's grief and forcing her to reevaluate her life.

In the first of her trilogy of inspiring memoirs, Dee recounts how, determined to heal from the pain and suffering that had darkened her world, she embarked on a spiritual quest, which eventually led her to quit her job and everything she'd known to start a new life in India with her young son.

Dying and the Art of Being
(Book 2 in *The Truth is Within* trilogy)

Navigating Our Fears Around Death, Dying and Endings of all Kind

Dee takes her story to a sleepy fishing village in South Goa, India, where she builds a new life for herself and her young son. But the brutal murder of a young Irish girl stops Dee in her tracks, calling her into the pain, suffering and injustices of the world, which triggers a deep remembrance inside.

In the second book of her trilogy, Dee invites the reader to explore the nature of reality through the death and dying process. She shares rare insights and wisdom from Tibetan Buddhism, alongside practical tips from her training with the Soul Midwives, who use ancient practices to assist those who are dying. As she wrote Book 2, she worked with a sacred oil called spikenard, which helped to expand her consciousness in preparation for her own near-death experience in Bali.